KINGDOM BUSINESS 101

: OCCUPY TILL I COME

I0490117

By MARCUS A. SHEFFIELD

FOUNDER AND PRESIDENT

Of

Tree of life Glorious Bible College

A message presented to the Church at large

Copyright © 2013 Sheffield Enterprise, Inc.

ISBN: 1484027191
ISBN-13: 978-1484027196

DEDICATION

I dedicate this book to my Dad who is my father twice, my mentor, and my friend.

And my Mother, Pauline Sheffield, one of the wisest women in the world, but not of the world. (A New Testament Woman)

BISHOP DR. JOHNNIE C. SHEFFIELD

December 30, 1927 – May 3, 2012

"For though you have countless guides in Christ, you do not have many fathers. For I became your father in Christ Jesus through the gospel."

A good man leaves an inheritance to his children's children. The knowledge goes to the children.

He was a visionary, a prophet, who saw a great change coming, a change which is upon us today. He believed that the people of God could do anything that they imagined to do, and soar as high as the mind of Christ can take you.

CONTENTS

Tree Of Life Glorious Bible College

A KINGDOM EXPANDING, FAITH BASED SCHOOL WITH A BUSINESS
APPROACH AND GLOBAL VISION IN COMMITTING THE GLORIOUS
GOSPEL TO FAITHFUL MEN AND WOMEN THAT WILL BE ABLE TO TEACH
OTHERS ALSO.

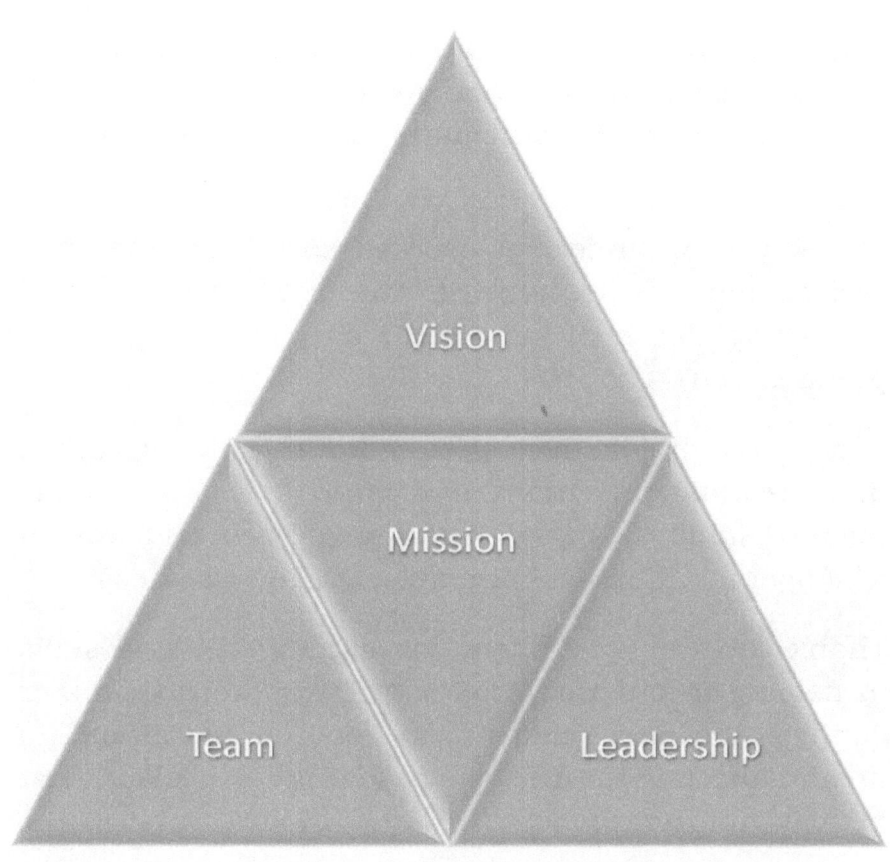

ACKNOWLEDGMENTS

In all thy ways acknowledge him, and He shall direct thy path.

Proverbs 3:6

To my support system and mastermind team, my wife Alyce, my sons, Marcus Anthony Jr., Jonathan Marc, Joel Asa, Justin Lamar and Maurice Walter, to my daughters, Marlyssa Rocine, Racheal Ifataya, Jocelynn Mariah, Jonia Michelle and Ashlynn Faith thank you for being one of the best parts of my life, my joy and my crown.

Thank you Maurice, you worked so diligently editing and adding your expertise to this project; you helped in making this book possible. I am very grateful and proud of you.

Every great project need a team, for insight, correction, proof reading, injections and etc... My team is my talented family along with the great men and women who operate in biblical principles and do business:

Thank you Deborah Shaw, for your talents and skills in helping to put this project together. To my brother Johnny Sheffield, thank you for reminding me to dream, and to write the vision, and make it plain, that he may run that readeth it.

Thank you again to all.

Abstract

This book represents an outward and inward approach to wealth creation as it pertains to the kingdom of God. The manuscript illustrates the importance of becoming financially independent in a growingly competitive globalized economy. The use of spiritual authority as well as economic theory and instruments are key components in Kingdom Business 101.

Your role in reading this is to take an introspective as well as a big picture approach of your personal finances, and how you can create a niche in this world. My goal is to reveal both spiritual and economic knowledge to foster financial intellectual growth in the mindset of the individual and the church as a whole.

I am assured that many will not accept the concept of this book. It goes against Traditional understandings of what we have been taught for generations. The information that we received was good for the time, but things have changed.

God is a progressive God, whose character never changes. The Word tells us that God said "For I am the LORD, I change not; also the writer of Hebrews said "Jesus Christ the same yesterday, and today, and forever." Even though His character never changes nor His attributes, but His methods change. If God's methods could not change, no doubt we would be scooping up dung from sacrificial animals that being under the law required. Also there was a change in the priesthood. Remember that man shall not live by bread alone, but by every Word that proceedeth out of the mouth of God. God's word is a proceeding Word. God is yet speaking today.

There was also a change from the agrarian age to the industrial age. And now we are in the information age. What worked in each of these ages may not be transferable to the next age. Many of you will not be able to release yourselves from outdated and antiquated thinking of a dying age. We are in a new age; I'm not speaking of a religion, but a time.

The first part of the book deals mainly with economic prospective. It encompasses the four states of economic conditions. In part I you will see a detailed description of the four quadrants of business. Part II details how to apply the segments of business in your economic life. You will find examples from the past and present, and how to take your experience and become more financially independent now. Finally the third part includes biblical authority and references of why it is important for the kingdom to become economically conscience today.

Keep in mind, we are to progress while yet being content, having food and raiment; but we are also to set goals and desire more out of life, while laying up for eternal life. The journey is just as important as the destination. If the Lord will, we shall live, and do this, or that.

Yet, mounting economic strain, increasing competition, and growing numbers of economic tools for wealth creation, many in the church are reluctant to change. We must take a big picture view of our economic conditions, and take advantage of financial avenues. With all these conditions will individuals in the church or the church itself take the first steps to becoming financially independent? You must ask yourself this question, "Will I take the first step toward financial independence?" Responding yes will empower you, and you will get much out of this book.

THERE'S A RECKONING COMING!

Scripture Text

St. Matthew 25: 14-30 *-for the kingdom of heaven is as a man travelling into a far country, who called his own servants, and delivered unto them his goods. And unto one he gave five talents, to another two, and to another one; to every man according to his several ability; and straightway took his journey. Then he that had received the five talents went and traded with the same, and made them other five talents. And likewise he that had received two, he also gained other two. But he that had received one went and dug in the earth, and hid his lord's money. After a long time the lord of those servants cometh, and reckoned with them. And so he that had received five talents came and brought other five talents, saying, Lord, thou deliveredst unto me five talents: behold, I have gained beside them five talents more. His lord said unto him, well done, thou good and faithful servant: thou hast been faithful over a few things, I will make thee ruler over many things: enter thou into the joy of thy lord. He also that had received two talents came and said, Lord, thou deliveredst unto me two talents: behold, I have gained two other talents beside them. His lord said unto him, well done, good and faithful servant; thou hast been faithful over a few things, I will make thee ruler over many things: enter thou into the joy of thy lord. Then he* *which had received the one talent came and said, Lord, I knew thee that thou art an hard man, reaping were thou hast not sown, and gathering were thou hast not strawed: and I was afraid, and went and hid thy talent in the earth: lo, there thou hast that is thine. His lord answered and said unto him, thou wicked and slothful servant, thou knewest that I reap were I sow not and gather were I have not strawed: thou oughtest therefore to have put my money to the exchangers, and then at my coming I should have received mine own with usury. Take therefore the talent from him, and give it unto him which hath ten talents. For unto every one that hath shall be given, and he shall have abundance: but from him that hath not shall be taken away even that which he hath. And cast ye the unprofitable servant into outer darkness: there shall be weeping and gnashing of teeth.*

St Luke 19:13- *And he called his ten servants: and delivered them ten pounds, and said unto them, Occupy till I come.*

St Matthew 20:7- *They say unto him, Because no man hath hired us. He saith unto them, Go ye also into the vineyard; and whatsoever is right, that shall ye receive.*

St Luke 2:49- *And he said unto them, How is it that ye sought me? Wist ye not that I must be about my Father's business?*

Psalms 66:12- *Thou hast caused men to ride over our heads; we went through fire and through water: but thou broughtest us out into a wealthy place.*

Introduction

According to the scriptures, Our Lord Jesus proclaimed occupy till I come. I believe that our duty to serve the kingdom means to become financially and spiritually free. The economic strains of today's turbulent post industrial conditions could dictate our well being and become an impediment to our potential. Because of those conditions, we must occupy or do business while we inhabit this earth to advance the Kingdom of God. The Kingdom of God should not only invade and advance our personal lives, but also our families, our church, our communities, also our government and the world.

God's people should share in financial prosperity. The 21st century economy contains dynamic aspects, yet most people today use 20th century techniques that stagnates ones earning power. To become financially free, working smarter rather than harder would be ideal. While the majority goes for the forty year plan, the wealthy pursue a four year plan. A four year plan that maximizes one's earning potential and power creates the ideal condition for economic prosperity.

It is true that 5% of the people share 95% of the wealth, while 95% of the people share 5% of the wealth. No wonder many people ascribe to the scarcity doctrine. The scarcity doctrine ideology implies that only so many pieces of the pie exist. This ideal has been ingrained in so many of our psyches. We must begin to see abundance. The Atlantic Ocean, so abundant with water is not affected whether you remove a thimble full or a ship load. Its vastness simply will not realize its absence.

Our Father whose riches are so prevalent that his streets are paved with gold, told us to ask what we will. God is our source and everything belongs to Him. God said "For every beast of the forest is mine, and the cattle upon a thousand hills. I know all the fowls of the mountains: and the wild beasts of the field are mine. If I were hungry, I would not tell thee: for the world is mine, and the fullness thereof." Also "The silver is mine, and the gold is mine, saith the LORD of hosts." He is the King of the kingdom, all of our gifts and talents and money belongs to Him, as well as we ourselves; we are his people and the sheep of His pasture. The Lord is my shepherd.

Even as we speak, the supposed middle class shrinks into non existence. Soon and very soon there will be no middle ground left to be divvied up, and you will have to make a conscience decision whether to be either rich (wealthy) or poor. Now do not get me wrong, God does not love the rich any more than the poor. There is no respecter of persons with God. Jesus said to his disciples "For ye have the poor always with you; but me ye have not always." However the poor is severely limited. The time is now for individuals to do business and make their path straight to prosperity. I am sure that each and every one of us would choose financial freedom.

The time of being burdened with crippling debt, stifled in back breaking laborious occupations, exists only in the past. Through new avenues of wealth creation everyone has the tools to occupy till he come, with the gifts, talents and money that He has given to each and every one of us and take our financial health into our own hands. Remember that the kingdom belongs to God (kingdom of God).

Now concerning progress and contentment, progression and contentment go hand in hand, you can be content, as the Word of God tells us to be; having food and raiment, while setting goals and desiring more out of life. The journey is just as important as the destination. No matter where you are in life at the present moment be content, not covetous, not in wanting, not high-minded, nor trusting in uncertain riches; but do good, be rich in good works, ready to distribute, willing to communicate; laying up in store for yourselves a good foundation against the time to come that you may lay hold on eternal life.

Follow after righteousness, godliness, faith, love, patience, meekness. Fight the good fight of faith, lay hold on eternal life. Learning to be content and trusting in the living God who gives us richly all things to enjoy.

St. Matthew 6:33- *But seek ye first the kingdom of God, and his righteousness; and all these things shall be added unto you.*

St Matthew 16:26- *For what is a man profited, if he gain the whole world, and lose his own soul? Or what shall a man give in exchange for his soul?*

Jeremiah 9:23-24- *Thus saith the LORD, Let not the wise man glory in his wisdom, neither let the mighty man glory in his might, let not the rich man glory in his riches: But let him that glorieth glory in this, that he understandeth and knoweth me, that I am the LORD which exercise lovingkindness, judgment, and righteousness, in the earth: for in these things I delight, saith the* **LORD.**

The LORD certainly wants us to profit, but not at the expense of our own souls. Save yourself first. Be saved and rich toward God yourself, because even if you are rich and if you preach the gospel and save the whole world, if you are not saved that would profit you nothing. The apostle Paul said in

1 Corinthians 9:27- *But I keep under my body, and bring it into subjection: lest that by any means, when I have preached to others, I myself should be a castaway.*

I do not want to be a cast away after I have preached to others. However it would profit us to gain the whole world and our own soul was saved also. Think win/win.

Nothing but the blood of Jesus; the Lamb of God, can redeem a man's soul, not silver nor gold.

1 Peter 1:18- *Forasmuch as ye know that ye were not redeemed with corruptible things, as silver and gold, from your vain conversation received by tradition from your fathers; But with the precious blood of Christ, as of a Lamb without*

blemish and without spot:

Romans 1:16- For I am not ashamed of the gospel of Christ: for it is the power of God unto salvation to every one that believeth; to the Jew first and also to the Greek.

In this dispensation of time God has designed that a person be saved through the foolishness of the preaching of the cross. For God so loved the World (every man, woman, boy and girl of all nations of people, the whole human race), that He gave his only begotten Son, that whosoever believeth in him should not perish, but have everlasting life.

Jesus Christ the last Adam (The Word was made flesh), who knew no sin, took upon himself all of our sins. For all mankind that was born in the first man Adam had sinned and came short of the glory of God. Therefore death had passed upon all men, for the wages of sin is death (eternal death).

Jesus Christ died on the cross (crucified), shedding his precious blood, being wounded for our transgressions, bruised for our iniquities, chastised for our peace and striped for our healing. He was buried in a borrowed tomb; his soul went to hell for three days and three nights to pay the full penalty of our sins. He rose from the dead after three days and three nights.

By his own blood he entered in once into the holy place (heaven), having obtained eternal redemption for us. To everyone that believeth, we have redemption and the forgiveness of our sins. He was seen of many witnesses after his resurrection. He ascended back to heaven, and came back as the Holy Ghost to empower the believer.

You must first hear the gospel, then you must believe the gospel (death, burial, and resurrection of Jesus Christ), next you must repent (change and realize that there is no other way to be saved except through Jesus Christ, and His shed blood), then you must be born of the water by being baptized in water in the name of Jesus Christ for the remission of your sins, Then receive the gift of the Holy Ghost (Free gift for believing. The initial evidence being; speaking with other tongues as the Spirit give you the utterance). Being born of the Spirit and receiving power to be a witness of Jesus Christ. Now you are a new creation.

Acts 2:38- *Then Peter said unto them, Repent, and be baptized every one of you in the name of Jesus Christ for the remission of sins, and ye shall receive the gift of the Holy Ghost.*

St. John 3:5- *Jesus answered, Verily, verily, I say unto thee, Except a man be born of the water and of the Spirit, he cannot enter into the kingdom of God.*

2 Corinthians 5:17- *Therefore if any man be in Christ, he is a new creature: old things are passed away; behold, all things are become new.*

3 John 2- *Beloved, I wish above all things that thou mayest prosper and be in health, even as thy soul prospereth.*

Even in times like these you can be content and progress at the same time. For I know and can boldly say The Lord is my helper and I will not fear what man shall do unto me.

Psalms 94:14- *For the Lord will not cast off his people, neither will he forsake his inheritance.*

St Matthew 28:20- *Teaching them to observe all things whatsoever I have commanded you: and, lo, I am with you alway, even unto the end of the world. Amen.*

Remember Israel in journeying out of Egypt into the wilderness; no shelter, no food, no water but God provided all these things. They set up camp in the wilderness and were being fed with manna from heaven (angel's food) and quail by the providence of God. They wanted to be content and complacent and stay in the wilderness, and some even wanted to go back to where they came from (Egypt), yet God wanted more for them. He wanted them to reach their full inheritance. God instructed them to move out of their comfort zone and into His full promises.

Even though, they would face an unwilling enemy. They must occupy their territory, conquer and settle in. The children of Israel let fear grip their hearts, which made them say things like, "we wish we were dead", "we are weak", "we are grasshoppers", "we are not able", "it's too big for us", "it must not be for us", "let's just stay where we are". The scriptures says, "But if God be for us, who can be against us?"

Will you go for the forty year plan as some of

the wilderness travelers or will you move when God say move into a greater inheritance?

Hebrews 6:3- *And this will we do, if God permit.*

When faced with unwilling and unyielding enemies as old mindsets and financial strains (the giants), keep moving forward. There is a promise land of more than enough. Let us possess the faith, courage, and obedience of Joshua and Caleb, which had another spirit and followed God fully, and lead this people forward into the plans of God. Godliness with contentment is great gain.

Moses the meekest man on the earth (not the weakest man), had already given some of the people of God an inheritance on the wilderness side of Jordan. He had captured the land from Sihon the king of the Amorites, and Og the king of Bashan. He gave their land as an inheritance unto the tribes of Rueben, Gad and the half tribe of Manasseh. However, before his death, he instructed them that they must go over the Jordan River armed and ready to do battle against the enemy, and help their brethren that had not possessed their inheritance as yet, which was on the other side of Jordan. God have an inheritance for each one of us, and we ought not to be satisfied until we all come into our full inheritance. Most of all we must rest in the finished work of The Lord Jesus Christ, a greater rest than what Joshua brought the people of God.

Hebrews 4:3- *For we which have believed do enter into rest, as he said, As I have sworn in my*

wrath, if they shall enter into my rest: although the works were finished from the foundation of the world.

1 Corinthians 10:24- *Let no man seek his own, but every man another's wealth.*

To become financially free, working smarter rather than harder would be ideal, however the majority will go for the forty year plan, but the wealthy will always pursue a four year plan. A four year plan that maximizes one's earning potential and power to create the ideal condition for economic prosperity.

Jeremiah 29:11-*"I know the thoughts that I think toward you, saith the Lord, thoughts of peace, and not of evil, to give you an expected end."*

Scriptures:

I Timothy 6:6-19   Hebrews13:56

Philippians 4:11,13

PART I

OCCUPY

TILL I COME

OCCUPY TILL I COME

(DO BUSINESS)

In the modern world, business is the driving force behind most of our lives. Although business' influential nature in our lives, it gives the impression of a secular word excluded from the church or kingdom. However business is considered a spiritual word which is much talked about throughout scripture. The word business itself only can be located a few times in scriptures, but the implied meaning of business is throughout. The word, occupy, which Jesus said till I come, means to do business.

The body of Christ is beginning to understand that not only are we to seek for jobs and job security, but it is spiritually correct to be business minded, and to have an entrepreneurial spirit.

The Four Quadrants (Paradigms) of Business

Robert Kiyosaki in his book titled "Rich Dads Cash flow Quadrant" states,

"There are four ways or quadrants in business in which a person can create income, or cash flow. They are as an employee, a small business owner, a big business owner, or as an investor. Also income can be earned, passive, or portfolio." At this point, we are not talking about inherited money, marrying for money, stealing, cheating, lying, embezzlement, breaking the law, tax evasion, finding money, robbery, etc. (begging and borrowing), giving, gifting, seedtime and harvest and favor which are other ways to obtain finance.

You will see in the following lesson that these four quadrants can also be considered four paradigms [1 an example or model 2. A generally accepted concept that explains a complex idea, set of data, methodology or theory etc.], or a world view. It takes a shift in your mindset, values and view in order to change paradigms (paradigm shift). Each quadrant is considered a paradigm. The employee operates from a paradigm, as well, the small business owner. It takes a complete shift in paradigms to operate as a big business owner or as an investor (insider, sophisticated, and accredited), for those that want to change. It is as going from a caterpillar to a butterfly (metamorphosis). Even though it is the same being, it is something altogether different. You may be the same individual, but a different person (transformed).

St. John 21:5-6- *Then Jesus saith unto them, Children, have ye any meat? They answered him, No. And he said unto them, Cast the net on the right side of the ship, and ye shall find. They cast therefore, and now they were not able to draw it for the multitude of fishes.*

2 Corinthians 5:17- *Therefore if any man be in Christ, he is a new creature: old things are passed away; behold, all things are become new.*

CHAPTER 1

Employee Quadrant

The E (employee) quadrant pertains to a person's earning power by selling his or her labor where the person earns income in the form of a paycheck or a *salary*. People from this quadrant work a job for an owner of a company. Whether the employee is the janitor or the president, their labor is owned by another individual. You might hear the person from this quadrant saying, "I'm looking for a safe, secure job with good pay and excellent benefits.

The person with earned income in the employee quadrant usually pays the highest percentage in taxes on the income that is received. Most times 50% goes to the government through social insurance taxes and other forms. Remember that employers are obligated to make payments to the government, and pay other expenses for having employees. These expenses includes, but is not limited to: workman's compensation, insurance, matching social insurance taxes, matching 401k contributions, federal and state unemployment taxes, and other costs associated with being an employer. For an example if it cost the company $8 per hour, per employee, they now can only pay $10 per hour instead of $18 per hour. Then there is also Federal, state and local income taxes that must be paid by the employee, as well as their portion of social insurance taxes, insurance and retirement.

That is why it's been said that employees are 50% partners with the government, and must take care of their expenses with after tax dollars. The government is concerned with the unemployment rate, not only for the sake of the unemployed, but also for their payday (taxes).

In the employee quadrant becoming wealthy can be very difficult or even forgotten. Cash flows from this quadrant simply are not adequate considering time spent to be considered the best vehicle to wealth. Instead of working for money, the wealthy educate their children to become financially free by having their money work for them. They achieve this by quickly converting their earned income into passive and portfolio income. Passive and portfolio income is the least taxed income, and in many cases tax free. (Passive and portfolio income will be explained later). In the E (employee) quadrant generally the harder one works or the higher one climbs the corporate ladder, the higher one will be taxed as their income climb.

The path that folks normally take that has been instilled in the majority of our psyches include: going to school, getting good grades, finding a job with a company with good pay and excellent benefits, and working that job harder and harder until retirement. This is employee quadrant advice.

Chapter 2

Small Business Quadrant

The second quadrant is the S quadrant, and stands for self employed, small business owner, or specialist. The S quadrant sometimes refers to smart people's or stars quadrant. The S quadrant contains many of the doctors, lawyers, accountants, consultants, ministers, real estate brokers, athletes, and movie stars. Almost every profession is included in this category such as: plumbers, restaurateurs, child care providers, property managers, landscapers, contractors, heating and air specialists, pest control companies, auto mechanics, barbers, massage therapists, and the list goes on. Anyone that sells their time for their specialty is S classers, mostly with fewer than five hundred employees.

However this quadrant has the highest amount of risk associated with it, and the taxes are just as high or higher than the employee quadrant, and the entrepreneur must work nonstop to keep the money flowing. Talk about if you don't work you don't eat, it is clearly shown in this quadrant. Only so many hours are in the day that a person can work, limiting the amount of money that could be generated.

The following can be heard from entrepreneurs in the S quadrant saying: if you want it done right, do it yourself, or my rate is $40 per hour, my normal commission rate is 7% of the total price, I got more than 30 hours into the project, or I can't seem to find people who want to work and do the job right. In contrast to the big business owners that usually have teams to organize and allocate responsibility; the small business owner is more liable for the work and debt. They are often seen as the John Wayne type of businessman. They're rugged individuals, their theme song being "I did it my way" and "I got to be me".

The small business owner is intensely involved with company affairs, micro-managing every detail of their prized company. These people cannot take too much time off unless finding someone suitable to the needs of their business.

There are a variety of responsibilities that small business owners take on. They must create systems encompassing everything associated with the business including: naming, branding, finding start-up capital, human resources, payroll, production, purchasing and vendors, accounts receivables, accounts payable, advertisement, marketing, sales, distribution, taxes, bookkeeping, accounting, engineering, inventory, buildings, maintenance, transportation, research and development, security, legal and government compliance, discipline, attitudes, lawsuits and developing company identity etc.

Some see small business owners as simply buying themselves a job, which never is expanded into big business. In big business a larger workforce is necessary, and is expanded to a greater array of locations and markets.

The S quadrant is commonly called the selfish quadrant. It is given this name because in big business you make money for stakeholders first, which include increasing share holders value (stocks). Whereas the small business owner focuses on themselves and in most cases are the highest paid. Nine out of ten small business owners are out of business within a five year span; and those that survive 90 percent are out of business in 10 years or just fooling themselves, not progressing.

Even many of the professional athletes are not immune to this statistic. Usually broke five years after ending their career, if they failed to become financially educated, and made sound cash flowing investments, the millions of dollars they made would mean nothing. Same with many of the lucky individuals that win mega millions in the lottery usually return to their same financial condition in a very short amount of time. Also many of the people that receive inheritances from the previous generation usually return back to their same financial condition. They are not able to increase it and pass it on to the next generation. This is proof that more money does not necessarily lead to financial freedom, financial education is the key. That is why the rich and the wealthy educate their heirs in financial knowledge, so that their wealth can continue trans-generational.

Ecclesiastes 2:18-19- *Yea, I hated all my labour which I had taken under the sun: because I should leave it unto the man that shall be after me. And who knoweth whether he shall be a wise man or a fool? Yet shall he have rule over all my labour wherein I have labored, and wherein I have shewed myself wise under the sun. This is also vanity*

A person working at McDonalds has the same opportunity for wealth as the high paid doctors and lawyers. It is not how much money that you make, but how much you keep, how much that money works for you and how many generations it exists.

An individual from the employee quadrant who strives to become an entrepreneur most likely will end up in the S (self-employed) quadrant. The title of big business owner is usually not attained due to steep entrance barriers. Still there are those who go from job to job/ pay check to pay check, all in the employee quadrant. Many fail to become financially independent and make lasting changes in their core values, allowing them to change quadrants (paradigm shift).

Financial freedom must start on the inside, in

our spirit, before the mind can make lasting changes. First is spirit (word), next soul (mind, will and emotions), then body (manifestation), or demonstration.

Although the employee class have the least financial freedom, employment can teach individuals important characteristic to succeed as a proprietor. Entrepreneurs usually take the path from the employee to the small business owner. From employee to entrepreneurship, the small business owner can learn the integrities of business (mission, team, leadership, cash flow, communication, systems, legal, and product). In the order of importance, notice that in these integrities (wholeness) of business that product comes last, because as we know many people have million dollar ideals, but fail to bring their product to market and make it successful. The reason is that they put the product first, without taking care of first things first. Ray Kroc, the founder of McDonalds stated "Most people can build a better hamburger than he could, but few could build a better system".

Also the entrepreneur can learn how to allocate time and effort to become most efficient. It provides them with a better understanding of how to create a more productive atmosphere for the financially dependent.

The job of the entrepreneur is to create jobs. Most of the jobs in the United States derive from small and big business. Business, not the government should be the driver of long lasting employment, so it is the task of the entrepreneur to create more jobs.

Therefore, the government gives tax breaks and grants to the entrepreneur and those that provide affordable housing and energy or take on projects that the government wants done. There will always be people that need jobs as all legitimate work is honorable in the sight of God. The person working at McDonalds can become wealthy, as well as the doctor and lawyer with financial knowledge.

CHAPTER 3

Big Business Quadrant

The third quadrant is the B quadrant or big business quadrant. It is classified as having at least 500 employees, usually uses a system, and has an operating structure specific to each firm. This is usually were the rich and the wealthy hang out. You might hear someone from this quadrant saying "I'm looking for a new president to run my company".

When starting a big business or corporation a person would take on considerably less risk individually, although in traditional big business there are significant entrance barriers. The vertical hieratical structure allows responsibility and liability to be spread throughout the company, unlike a sole proprietorship, partnerships, general partnerships and many small businesses which responsibility and risk is shared between one or two people.

The biggest responsibility in a corporation is to increase share holders wealth. The leadership officers are obligated to act in the best interest of their investors. Companies keep investors satisfied by producing healthy financial statements, which in return bolster their reputation increasing their stock price per share. Companies use the balance sheet, income statement, and statement of cash flows to evaluate their quarterly financial performance. The stock price is essentially how much confidence investors have in a company to perform and have steady growth. In a public corporation each share holder has a say about the company's objective based on their percentage of shares.

Not commonly known, network marketing is included in big business. It is considered big business because while the network marketer is not an employee, but a business owner, those associated with them could be well over 500 people. Network marketing is called the new personal franchise system, as a person can outperform traditional franchises. By collaborating, communicating, and building networks and interconnected systems, individuals can create vast riches gaining their financial freedom. Most of the overhead and management of the business that qualifies it as big business is already done.

The greatest advantage of a network marketing company is the low cost of entering the business, meaning that almost any ordinary person could do network marketing. Although the low entry cost is a great advantage, it is also a disadvantage, if the networker feels that it is not a great investment, and would not be serious about it like he would if it involved his life savings. Also the training in sales that is received is priceless. It could cost several hundreds of thousands of dollars to get into traditional franchises, causing adverse conditions for most in the working class to enter.

The story of Ray Kroc, the founder of McDonald's; is often told when referring to big business. In a commencement speech he gave to a graduating class, he asked the class what kind of business was he in. The class almost unanimously responded restaurant, hamburgers, French fries, etc. Ray Kroc simply shook his head and commenced to enlighten the graduates of his business strategy. He submitted that yes he sells hamburgers, but his real business is real estate. Kroc stated that most can build a better hamburger than he could, but few could build a better system than he could. And the real estate that is under a McDonald's restaurant becomes most valuable and the business could be run by teenagers and the elderly.

The difference between small and big business is as vast as the ocean is wide. Even Thomas Edison was not the first to create the light bulb, but he was the first to create a system for the light bulb's usage by many consumers.

One account of the contrast of big business to small business is seen in the following common story.

This is about someone who developed a personal franchise system (big business).

Some while ago I heard a great story about a quaint village that was self sufficient and happy. Although they were blissful they had one problem [find a problem to solve and you could find your niche]. They didn't have any water supply in the village, and the village was a mile or so away from the lake. This made it burdensome to acquire the necessary water for everyday use as rain was scarce. They decided to advertise for someone to solve this problem by taking bids for the project to have water delivered to them on a daily basis. Two people volunteered. They decided to award the contract to both of them to increase competition to assure a fair price and a back up supply of fresh water.

Immediately Ed, which was one of the awardees of the contract, went out and bought two galvanized buckets. Soon he was running back and forth to the lake and filling his buckets with water emptying them into a large holding tank in the village built for storing excess water. From morning to dusk Ed worked diligently. Each morning he was up before the villagers, and worked making his days worth.

Bill the other contractor disappeared for awhile; he was not seen for months. Ed was glad because he was making all the money. However Bill was hard at work making a business plan, and creating a corporation. He found four investors, and employed a president to handle the business. Bill returned six months later with a construction crew. Within the year

Bill built a large stainless steel pipeline, connecting the village to the lake. Bill had a grand opening celebration and announced that his water was much cleaner than Ed's. He boasted that he could supply water 24/7/365 at 75% less per unit. The villagers rejoiced and began to exclusively use Bill's pipeline.

Now Ed lowered his prices by 75%, and bought 4 more buckets. He then bought covers for the buckets, because the villagers complained that dirt was getting into Ed's water. He hired his two sons to carry the other four buckets, and to work the night shift, and weekends. Ed's kids went off to college, Ed promising them that someday this business will be theirs, but for some reason his children never returned. Ed hired employees and they eventually had union problems. They wanted higher wages, more benefits, and they only wanted to carry one bucket.

On the other hand Bill expanded his system to other villages. He rewrote his business plan and was off selling his high speed, high volume, low cost, and clean water delivery system to villages throughout the world. He was solving problems for people for pennies per bucket, delivering billions of buckets of water every day. He makes money regardless if he works or not. Billions of people consume billions of buckets of water, money pours into his bank account. Not only does he have a pipeline to deliver water, but money as well. Bill and all of his descendants lived happily ever after. Ed toiled endlessly for the rest of his life having continuous financial problems.

The end.

<u>CHAPTER 4</u>

Investors Quadrant

The fourth and last is the (I) quadrant or the investors quadrant. Investors leverage their capital to make money work for money. The investors quadrant is the envy of all the other quadrants. You might hear the investor saying "Is my cash flow based on an internal rate of return or net rate of return". It is important that not only the investor receive a return **on** investment, but a return **of** investment. The investor must be adept at leveraging money, and raising capital. This will be explained in greater detail when reviewing OPM (other people's money).

Passive income is generated from real assets such as investment real estate, interest, dividends, businesses, royalties, brands, licensing, commodities, residuals, and anything that produces income without continual working. Passive income, being the least strenuous way to create wealth, should be a focal point to anyone striving to become financially independent.

For instance, if an investor invested in real estate and rented it out. No doubt the tenant's monthly rental payments would pay for the mortgage, PITI (principal, interest, taxes and insurance), expenses, utilities, maintenance, management and security of the property. After the expenses were paid, the remaining money would belong to the investor and be considered passive income. As Robert Kiyosaki points out in most of his books his rich dad taught him that a successful strategy to wealth creation is found in the game of Monopoly (four green houses, one red hotel). A business running without the owner working or with leverage this is also called passive income.

Investors also generate wealth through capital gains, which include stocks, bonds, and treasury bills. In the United States investment monies earned or capital gains is taxed at a considerable less rate. While a salary can be taxed up to 35% (+), the tax on capital gains is only 15% (plus social insurance taxes). A decreased tax rate allows investors to circulate their capital freer and faster. There are also legal ways that capital gains taxes can be deferred through a 1031 tax exchange.

Investing for capital gains (buying low and selling high or flipping properties) have been seen to be risky, especially when the real estate bubble busted, and properties lost value. Many house flippers were left holding the bag. A property need to be valuable when you buy it, a stock need to pay a dividend when you buy it. Even if it never appreciates it should produce a cash flow (profit after all expenses are paid).

One good strategy is to refinance your rental property and pull enough finance out to fund your next cash flowing project, doing this is the tax free way. Remember, that the rental income should cover all expenses, including the refinancing (tax free money), as well as produce a cash flow (passive income). This allows investors to increase their income greater than any wage paying job can. The rich and the wealthy teach their children to go after this type of income.

PART II

DOING BUSINESS IN THE MODERN AGE

DOING BUSINESS
IN THE MODERN AGE

At the dawn of the 20th century, industry spawned a boom in the economy, thus creating an abundance of secure well paying employment. New technology allowed greater division in labor adding even greater numbers of jobs. The use of the assembly line vastly increased efficiency while reducing the amount of skills that each worker needed to perform their assigned task. The automobile factories, the steel mills and coal mines, the rubber industry, as well the oil and gas fields experienced a great boom. Also there was an expansion in government jobs.

The church grew hand in hand with this industrial boom. These plentiful low skilled jobs and management positions were filled by many of the people in the church. Soon the people as well as many in the church depended on these types of jobs to sustain their middle class lifestyles.

Since the beginning of the industrial revolution to now, the world has changed as much as a caterpillar to a butterfly (metamorphosis). In this era innovation as well as a globalized economy greatly reduced the need for industrial age labor. New technology allowed one person to do a job that previously took four. Due to the reduction of power and influence of labor unions after the Reagan administration, it made it easier for manufactures to reduce benefits, erase job security, and allowed them to ship jobs across seas.

In this information age the church must abandon industrial age thinking. The world is vastly different than what it was forty years ago, and we must change with it (we are in the world, but not of the world).

Romans 12:2- *And be not conformed to this world: but be ye transformed by the renewing of your mind, that ye may prove what is that good, and acceptable, and perfect, will of God.*

CHAPTER 5

Industrial Age vs. Information Age

Common day practices dictate that we must attend school and receive good grades to be successful. Finding a secure job with benefits that would take care of you all of your life was good advice for the industrial age. However the same methods in the information age are less reliable and less effective. The same factories and manufacturing businesses that expanded the American middle class are rapidly evaporating.

The American dream of a three bedroom house, two vehicles, wife, two and a half children, and dog is disappearing as fast as winter snow in the spring heat. As a matter of fact many of the industrial age fortune 500 companies are changing by slashing and shipping jobs overseas. Many of these companies have gone to cheaper labor markets. They are becoming more efficient through innovation, meaning they can do the same job with a fourth of the workforce. New fortune 500 companies are emerging in the information age. Companies such as Apple, Google, Wal-Mart, Amazon, Facebook and network marketing companies are a few examples of the potential of information age industry.

The employee quadrant belief to strive for job security has been ingrained through the school system. The school system is based in the employee quadrant, providing our youth with little knowledge or financial education to take advantage of many of the information age opportunities, that extend beyond the employee and small business quadrant.

The American school system was borrowed from the Prussian Empire system which primary goal was to train its subjects for uniform labor and to be obedient soldiers. That is why little if anything is taught about financial education (knowledge), or how to be a big business owner or investor. In most cases we are taught only to be an employee for big business.

Their idea of financial education (economics) is to save money, be an informed consumer, balance a checkbook, create a budget, pick common stocks that corporations sell and turn your money over to so call financial experts to buy mutual funds, and invest for the long term. Financial education goes much further than our current school system teaches and college as well.

Remember that during slavery in the United States, it was illegal even to teach a slave how to read and write to prevent him from improving his lot in life. It should be no wonder to us that there is yet a conspiracy going on to keep the masses ignorant of financial knowledge.

Hosea 4:6- *My people are destroyed for lack of knowledge: because thou hast rejected knowledge, I will also reject thee, that thou shalt be no priest to me: seeing thou hast forgotten the law of thy God, I will also forget thy children.*

A formal education (academic, professional) in the information age is important, but it also should include financial knowledge as well. I thank God for the education that I have received, and I am very proud of the education that my family and my children have received, but it does not define your financial life as it did in the past. Many big business pioneers has emerged without being formally educated. Innovators such as Bill Gates, Henry Ford, Steve Jobs, Mark Zuckerberg, Thomas Edison, and Walt Disney are just a few who dropped out of college. Instead of pursuing employee quadrant occupations, they focused their skills on big business, and employed formally trained people to make money for them. Remember that it is more important to work smarter rather than harder in the information age.

Also I must say that I thank God for our soldiers, who protect our land and the freedoms that we enjoy. Many of my family members are and were members of the armed forces. I myself served for a short time.

During the industrial age the pension plans were defined benefit plans. Now most pension plans are defined contribution plans, requiring one to invest in their retirement through a 401k plan. These 401k plans have been seen to be some very risky investments. Without financial education ordinary people have become investors. 401k funds are turned over to financial brokers who benefit whether money is generated for investors or not. (Many brokers are not investors, and the reason they are called brokers is because they are broker than you). Only a short time ago the stock market fell 777 points and lost 1.2 trillion dollars of the investor's money, making it the worst down slide since the great depression.

Remember that while some investors were losing money, the inside, sophisticated and the accredited investors were making money. The only time the majority of the people who invest in the 401k plan make money, is when the stock market is going up. But the other investors (inside, sophisticated, and accredited) make money no matter how the market is moving, whether it is up, down or sideways.

Instead of having an investor's mentality, most investors in the 401k plan view themselves as savers. As the markets plummeted, the mainstream advice coming from the financial world, that benefit from these plans was to hold, pray, diversify and invest for the long term, when in fact, they themselves invest for the short term.

They say to diversify, yet many employee quadrant investors only possess paper assets in their portfolio. True, diversification means investing in multiple streams of income. These steams can include earned, paper, real estate, commodities and businesses. True diversification build ones passive income, money that you do not keep working for but money working for you, having multiple streams of income.

Genesis 2:10-14- *And a river went out of Eden to water the garden; and from thence it was parted, and became into four heads. The name of the first is Pison: that is it which compasseth the whole land of Havilah, where there is gold; and the gold of that land is good: there is bdellium and the onyx stone. And the name of the second river is Gihon: the same is it that compasseth the whole land of Ethiopia. And the name of the third river is Hiddekel: that is it which goeth toward the east of Assyria. And the fourth river is Euphrates.*

CHAPTER 6

Good Debt vs. Bad Debt

Deuteronomy 8:18- *But thou shalt remember the Lord thy God: for it is he that giveth thee power to get wealth, that he may establish his covenant which he sware unto thy fathers, as it is this day.*

The messages from the pulpits have been telling the body of Christ, for some time now, to remove all debt. I believe the kind of debt that we've been told to remove is bad debt. Bad debt and bad expenses are the liabilities that siphon money out of our pockets without giving us a real return on our investments. Bad debt is debt that is used to buy what Robert Kiyosaki calls doo-dads and liabilities in his #1 New York Times bestselling and #1 personal finance book of all time "Rich Dad Poor Dad".

There is nothing wrong with buying doo-dads, liabilities or the luxuries of life. The problem is that if bought with debt, and paid for with the money that is earned from the employee quadrant, it could lead to some financial struggles. Without a good budget the emergencies, or unforeseen events that occur in our lives, would not be sufficient. The typical American on average spends $1.22 for every one dollar that is earned. Most so called financial experts are telling the people to cut up their credit cards and live below their means. It would be more empowering and make more sense to inform people of how to expand their means.

My new understanding suggests that I not say that I could not afford something, because the moment you say that, immediately your mind shuts down. However if you say, how can I afford it? Immediately your sub-conscience and your spirit go to work to bring your mind the answer.

Furthermore the messages from the pulpits have not emphasized getting into good debt. I believe the body of Christ could benefit from good debt. Good debt is debt that places money into our pockets just like an asset. An asset puts money into our pockets whereas a liability takes money out of our pockets. Even the house that we live in is a liability and not an asset as we've been told, since it takes money out of our pockets. While it is good to own your own home, it is not good to call a liability an asset. The so call financial experts are telling the people to buy a bigger house, especially when the person receives a raise on their job, for tax reasons, and tax breaks. However, it would make more sense to first buy an asset that could pay for my liabilities. The wealthy usually buys liabilities and luxuries last, whereas the middle class buys them first, without buying an asset to pay for them. The poor usually own few liabilities and only pay for expenses (bills).

For example, if the banks money is used to make money it is considered good debt. If 10% is put down on a rental investment property, and the bank puts in 90%, and the tenant pays for the mortgage (an engagement till death) and expenses, the profit is received by the investor (passive income), this is good debt. [The appreciation on the property, the depreciation (phantom cash), the tax advantages, the amortization and every other plus goes to the investor instead of the bank; making the return on investment (roi) many times greater than 50% which is a lot better than earning 1%-5% in a traditional savings account].

Many businesses have used good debt to develop multiple streams of income. Leveraging good debt is part of business. Industrialists, retailers, big businesses, small businesses, and real estate developers use good debt to grow their assets. $100,000 could leverage $1,000,000, where more could be done with less. The true Capitalists forms Corporations and uses OPM (**O**ther **P**eople's **M**oney), OPT (**O**ther **P**eople's **T**ime and talents) and OPC (**O**ther **P**eople's **C**redit).

Bad debt has caused many good people to get into trouble causing them to lose their possessions and ruin their credit. With devalued credit, individuals cannot deal properly in good debt. Low scores from the credit bureau disqualify many from these money making ventures, this has to be dealt with. It's been said that only an extra $200 to $400 per month could be a solution to many peoples' financial problems, instead of filing bankruptcy.

Another solution to overcoming bad credit is adopting the thinking and actions of a true capitalist. Forming a corporation and using OPC, OPM and OPT can allow most to implement good debt. This sound like being a user, however instead of being counted out one must realize their mistake, get up, and move forward.

Life is set up that one learn from their mistakes, as a matter of fact some things cannot be learned except that the person is willing to fail. Look at the baby learning to walk, the child learning to ride a bike, or the Wright brothers at Kitty Hawk and the entrepreneur starting a new business after failure.

In the school system of today, students are punished for making mistakes, and for working together (this is called cheating). It is no wonder why so much rugged individualism exists in our society and many refuse to work together. Also it is why many are afraid to take any risks for fear of making a mistake, and why there is so much competing going on. We compete for grades, colleges, scholarships, jobs, positions, promotions, men against women, church against church. The scripture discourages this type of behavior but encourages team work.

II Corinthians 10:12- *"For we dare not make ourselves of the number, or compare ourselves with some that commend themselves: but they measuring themselves by themselves, and comparing themselves among themselves are not wise."*

One should have luxuries in life, driving the car and living in the house of their dreams. One strategy is to pay for luxuries with cash flowing assets in the form of passive income instead of earned income. For example, my rental house could pay for my dream car and when the car is paid off, I still have the car and the asset that produced the cash flow. I use to say in my confessions "I am out of debt, my needs are met and I have plenty more to put in store." I now say "I am out of bad debt and into good debt; my needs are met and I have plenty more to invest." With this type of mind set anything is possible. By forming corporations, eliminating bad debt, and implementing good debt, or by using OPM, OPT, OPC, you can gain financial freedom and afford any luxury you desire.

Usually the poor and the middle class insist on property and possessions being in their own name. However the rich and the wealthy doesn't want anything in their own name; on paper they are poor, this is a great business strategy because of the type of society that we live in, this is a litigious (suing, lawsuits) society, and a lot of people are trying to get something for nothing. The wealthy usually use the protection of a C corp., S corp., or a LLC (Limited Liability Company).

Many CEO's from the employee quadrant receive high salaries and perks. While on the other hand, the owner of the big business company usually receives a low salary, sometimes as low as $1.00/year, because they are building an asset and trans-generational wealth (preferred stock, dividends). This is also a great tax strategy.

CHAPTER 7

Rejection and Sales

From the womb babies are natural born salespersons. We start out with the mindset that we can have anything we want, even if it takes whining and crying. Through our unrelenting persistence we usually get what we want regardless of the amount of rejection. However, we are coaxed out of our persistence through the hard realities of life. To become successful the persistent trait must be relearned. We are told to stop asking and nagging, stop complaining, and stop being a pest. Through this we learn to stop selling and accept rejection.

To most the perception of a salesman is a middle aged sweaty balding man wearing cheap suits, bad cologne, and always cracking a duplicitous smile.

Uncommonly known a salesperson is one of the most successful and highest paid professions in the world. The fear of rejection is what encumbers many from pursuing a sales position; however the most reputable people in the world has once in their lives been rejected.

The reason why some nations and individuals are barely getting by and scraping from the bottom of the barrels is because they perceive that they have nothing to sell and are too afraid of being rejected.

Our Lord Jesus Christ, a man of sorrows, and acquainted with grief; was despised and rejected of men. He came unto his own and his own received him not; but as many as received him, gave he the power to become the sons of God. He was wounded for our transgressions, he was bruised for our iniquities: the chastisement of our peace was upon him; and with and by his stripes we are and were healed. Being crucified on the cross, He said Father forgive them for they know not what they do. We must deal with rejection and gain knowledge without blaming, justifying or arguing.

Reverend Dr. Martin Luther King Jr., admired by millions as a pillar for hope and dignity; was deeply rejected and hated. His assassination was a testament to the level of opposition he faced, yet he persevered pressing his agenda. He became a beacon for the truth in pointing out the errors in society, becoming the voice for the downtrodden and disenfranchised.

Sometimes it is dangerous to have a dream. Look at Joseph, the son who wore the coat of many colors. His brothers pronounced, "Behold this dreamer cometh." Joseph's dreams caused him to be stripped of his beautiful coat, a coat which was a representation of his authority. Then his brothers threw him into a pit without water, sold him as a slave (for 20 pieces of silver), dipped his coat in blood (a vesture dipped in blood), and lied to his father Jacob. Joseph was sold again into Egypt, made overseer over Potiphars' household, and then he was lied on and thrown into jail, being innocent.

Being blessed, Joseph's dreams were God inspired, and his gifts made room for him. Dreams that would take a person from the pit to the palace are what Joseph had. Eventually his dreams allowed him to become prime minister and ruler of the most powerful nation on the earth. As Our Lord Jesus Christ and Dr. Martin Luther King Jr. forgave their oppressors without violence, Joseph also forgave his brothers for they did not know what they were doing.

Before Joseph died, he made the children of Israel sware, saying God will surely visit you, and ye shall carry up my bones from hence. They were not to leave them in Egypt, but take them with them when they go back to the promise land some four hundred years later. This is what the future generation did.

Exodus 13:19- *And Moses took the bones of Joseph with him: for he had straitly sworn the children of Israel, saying, God will surely visit you; and ye shall carry up my bones away hence with you.*

These could have quit when encountering obstacles, but they looked into the eyes of rejection and endured. The lesson from our Lord is to keep sowing the seed (word) and eventually some will fall on good ground and bring forth fruit. Some thirty, some sixty and some one hundred fold. The good soil that received the seed and yielded a harvest, also endured all the calamities of the other soils. This good soil endured marauding birds (usually a picture of the enemy at work), scorching sun, and the dangers of encroaching weeds and thorns. In spite of these tests and trials, a harvest grew. This is not just 30%, 60%, and 100%, but the word fold means one hundred; so that's 3,000%, 6,000%, and 10,000%. This is a great return on your investment.

Genesis 26:12- *Then Isaac sowed in that land, and received in the same year a hundredfold: and the Lord blessed him.*

Rejected most times by the majority of the population, The President of the United States is often faced with a great deal of opposition. Looking at the odds there would be little reason why anyone would want to become president. One president that epitomized rejection was Abraham Lincoln. Lincoln was not a common politician. He was a compassionate morally sound president whose word was as solid as gold, which is why we call him honest Abe.

One of the founders of the Republican Party, he took a strong stance against the institution of slavery. It was a system which subjected millions of Africans to a life of endless and meaningless labor, against their will and freedom. He once said, "A house turned against itself cannot stand." Once the southern states declared their succession, Lincoln would face the ultimate test. To reunite the Union he would face not only opposition from the south, but also from officials within his own party and cabinet.

In the end the country was reunited, but at a horrific cost. Spanning over five years the Civil war cost as much in American blood as any other American conflict. There were many moments were Lincoln could have punched in his ticket and accept rejection. Many times the horrific death toll from battles such as Antietam, Fredericksburg, and Gettysburg could have made a weaker man falter.

Many felt that they were fighting a war with no end and that no one understood, but Lincoln did understand. He understood that this country needed to be whole to be great. He also knew that the evils of slavery could not continue. He was ready for the task of fulfilling his ambitions. Even though it would cost a generations blood, He knew that his mission and goals were just.

That makes you think about what if. What if Lincoln would have quit without a fight? What if he never saw his dream to the end? What if he never signed the emancipation proclamation? That really makes you think about what kind of world we would live in today without Lincoln, and the importance of overcoming rejection. To Lincoln rejection (equaled) success. Even though most could not see his vision, he persevered with or without their acceptance.

The more you can be rejected the richer and more successful you can become. The greater amount of rejection you receive the greater amount of knowledge you ascertain to remedy your errors. When rejected, we then learn from the experience and become better from it.

The Coca Cola brand is known throughout the world. Their nonstop advertising and marketing has ingrained their product in our minds for generations. By receiving feedback from the world they can continually improve their company.

Many can remember the blunder of new Coke. Coca Cola introduced a new coke with a revamped recipe for the new age. From emerging competition from companies like Pepsi Co., Coca Cola's growth stagnated. Thinking that the new taste of coke would reinvigorate old patrons and bring new drinkers to Coke, they pushed for the change. Unfortunately their test groups and high powered marketers were wrong. Consumers valued Cokes original and traditional taste over the trend of the time.

Almost unanimously rejected, Coca Cola company officials scrambled to pull the despised beverage from the isle, and reintroduce classic Coke, which sent their profits soaring through the roof. From this blunder the Coca Cola Company learned an invaluable lesson about their consumers. They were taught a significant lesson from their rejection, hopefully never to be repeated.

Getting breakfast to the table convinces us of

the importance of commerce. Imagine if we had to do everything ourselves. From raising the chickens to get the eggs, growing the wheat to bake bread, raising pigs for bacon and sausage (or raise turkeys), grow orange trees to get juice, and owning a cow for milk and the butter, and what about the seasonings? The significance of commerce is evident; we rely on others to sale us the best and most price efficient products available, this is the way of our society.

Once upon a time there was a big banker whose riches were vast and spread far and wide. One day he looked out of his towering office building. He peered over the city at the masses scrambling around and the many businesses operating. He looked with marveled eyes and said, "Look at all these people who work for me." This story tells us how in our society we all work for each other's benefit. Through commerce we all are connected and we all are salesmen of our craft.

Our lives are dominated by commerce which is as prevalent as sunshine. Sales are a key component in our commerce driven life. Think about it, look around, everything we possess is sold to us in some way. All the trinkets in our homes, the clothes we wear, the food we eat, the car we drive, the home we live in, and even our spouses are all linked to sales. Daily we are selling ourselves to convince others of our commitment, value, and talents. Whether it is selling a trivial appliance or our companionship, rejection and sales are essential parts of life.

CHAPTER 8

The 99 Percent vs. The 1%

To occupy means to take possession of by settlement or seizure, to hold possession of, to dwell in, to hold, to take up, and to employ. It also means to conquer, take over, invade, remain, take tenancy, reside, live in, pervade, command, extend, control, maintain, engage, monopolize and to do business. Occupy sounds a lot like

Genesis 1:28- *And God blessed them, and God said to them, Be fruitful, and multiply, and replenish the earth, and subdue it: and have dominion over the fish of the sea, and over the fowl of the air, and over every living thing that moveth upon the earth.*

The streets, the parks, the government centers

and Wall Street were filled with protesters from all walks of life from Main Street America, that are professing to be the 99%, who have been left out in the cold from the mainstream wealth. This wealth has been created for many banks and big businesses that simply have not trickled down to the people who are in the greatest need in these turbulent economic days. Not only are these demonstrations going on in the main cities and economic squares of the United States, but also in other nations throughout the world.

Unemployment is at an all time high, when you consider the underemployed, and the indigent who most of the times are not even counted, and they that are off the unemployment role, and those in the prisons, making the unemployment percentage far greater than the great depression era.

With this turbulent economic condition congress fails to act on passing any kind of jobs bill that would stimulate the economy out of the recession. That is why the 99 percenters need to change their mindsets on wealth creation. If the rich takes advantage of many of these avenues, then why cannot the rest of us. We in the 99 percent must be proactive in our economic life to see the types of financial independence that the wealthy and affluent enjoy.

Poverty can be considered an addiction. The reasons why I feel it is an addiction is the following: It is structurally ingrained in our lives, it is inherited, and you must first make a conscience decision to relieve yourself from it. There is a difference between being poor and broke, than in poverty. Broke is temporary, but poverty is eternal (we have been redeemed from poverty). Many in the church are not immune from the poverty addiction.

For many years the church discouraged financial gains beyond the employee quadrant. According to scripture, it is written, For the love of money is the root of all evil: it did not say that money itself is the root of all evil (money answereth all things, money is a defense). My understanding of this scripture makes me believe that the lack of money and the lack of financial freedom could lead to the love of money and is a factor to all kinds of evil. People in poverty could love money, remember that you cannot serve God and mammon (constantly focusing on need, greedy pursuit and worship of riches). I have seen the most rational caring people turn to evil acts because of the desperation of poverty. I have heard some say that they would do anything for money. I have seen many people spend money that should not be spent in the pursuit of winning the lottery, especially when the stakes go up. Talk of being creative, I have seen some witty inventions because of the need of money.

It takes money to be legally compliant with all the laws of the land; such as paying all of our taxes (income, real estate, personal, business, ad valorem, automobile, etc), insurances (health, life, automobile, property, real estate), debts (school loans, liabilities, personal loans, bills, contracts, etc.), child support, licenses and the list goes on. That is why in Old Testament times, poverty is written as a curse. We have been redeemed from poverty, sickness, disease and spiritual death.

Poverty = Want of earthly goods, destitution, pennilessness, penury, indigence, pauperism, want, need, insufficiency, starvation, famine, privation, insolvency, broken fortune, straits, scantiness, deficiency, meagerness, aridity, sparingness, stint, depletion, emptiness, vacancy, deficit, debt, wolf at the door, pinch, bite, tough going, lack, shortage, inadequacy, scarcity.

Galatians 3:13-14,29 *Christ hath redeemed us from the curse of the law, being made a curse for us: for it is written, Cursed is every one that hangeth on a tree: That the blessing of Abraham might come on the Gentiles through Jesus Christ; that we might receive the promise of the Spirit through faith. And if ye be Christ's, then are ye Abraham's seed, and heirs according to the promise.*

It is simple, we in the church must rise together as one to throw off poverty and advance the kingdom of God. Some believe that Jesus was poor and lived in poverty monetarily wise, but even when Jesus was a child, kings came from the east and the uttermost parts of the earth, and it was more than three kings, and they knew who he really was (God manifested in the flesh), for God had revealed it unto them. They presented him with gold (real money), not just a .50 cent piece, frankincense and myrrh (valuable commodities). If the Queen of Sheba and others brought treasures to Solomon and the half had never been told, then what about Jesus? Behold a greater that Solomon is here [Jesus Christ is the King of kings (THE LORD GOD)]. Take note, Moses, Job, Abraham,

Isaac, Jacob, Joseph, David, Solomon and Jesus, and many, many more were all millionaires (according to their time). They are the millionaires of the Bible.

From the great recession ordinary folks have lost their jobs, homes, life savings, and retirement funds. Although all the rules have been followed by those in question, the enigma that we call the economy has claimed their security without regret. From witnessing life securities dissipate due to foreclosures, bankruptcies, and decreasing 401ks while the few (1%) flourish, it should teach the 99 percent a valuable lesson. That lesson being that we can no longer accept only what they hand to us. If we continue to follow outdated economic theories we will carry on being ignored and violated.

Congregating masses are attempting to be heard and force a change in how government and financial institutions view them, but protest without action is useless. The civil rights protests were successful because folks were willing to take a stand through action. Complaining to stubborn financial institutions and governmental entities is a useless conquest. Government officials work hand in hand with financial institutions to keep the masses just content enough and fed. Action through our financial and monetary decisions is what speaks the loudest in a free market economy.

If we in the 99 percent became financially free from the big corporations, their misdeeds would have little consequence on our well being. The industrial revolution tied folks in the 99 percent ever so close to corporation, and for a while it was a mutually beneficial relationship. Like many relationships there is a time that you must call it quits. How many more black eyes must be sustained while living under the thumb of corporate America? If we work together with our fellow man and trust in God we can relinquish tyranny and take grasp of financial freedom.

Also you must begin to realize that most of the corporate world is good and honest, with a few bad. Even though the bottom line is profit and an increase in shareholders wealth, and usually when there is a reduction in the work force, the price of their stock goes up. Yet they are providing a great service to our society by creating jobs for those that need them. However the media sometimes portrays corporate America as evil based on a few. The banks was also created to make you rich, not poor. We must learn how to use the banks to our advantage, like the true capitalist.

The reason why some folks pass on many money making opportunities is that somehow they feel that making more money than you actually need is evil; or that an affluent life style is forbidden, that there is virtue in being poor, or that they would love money. They have been watching too much television and have bought into the lie that corporations, banks, and the rich are inheritantly evil. Contrariwise, some of the richest people in the world do the most good, they are the most generous, while many of the poor, and the middle class only think about themselves, and their immediate families, only their local churches and favorite charities. Remember that I said many, not all.

Your money should have a mission.

1 Timothy 6:17-19- *Charge them that are rich in this world, that they be not highminded, nor trust in uncertain riches, but in the living God, who giveth us richly all things to enjoy; That they do good, that they be rich in good works, ready to distribute, willing to communicate; Laying up in store for themselves a good foundation against the time to come, that they may lay hold on eternal life.*

Proverbs 19:17- *He that hath pity upon the poor lendeth unto the LORD; and that which he hath given will he pay him again.*

Matthew 25:40- *And the King shall answer and say unto them, Verily I say unto you, Inasmuch as ye have done it unto one of the least of these my brethren, ye have done it unto me.*

Matthew 26:11- *For ye have the poor always with you; but me ye have not always.*

Acts 20:35- *I have shewed you all things, how that so laboring ye ought to support the weak, and to remember the words of the Lord Jesus, how he said, it is more blessed to give than to receive.*

PART III

OCCUPY

CHAPTER 9

Blessed To Be a Blessing

Genesis 12:1-3 *Now the Lord had said unto Abram, get thee out of thy country, and from thy kindred, and from thy father's house, unto a land that I will show thee: And I will make of thee a great nation, and I will bless thee, and make thy name great; and thou shalt be a blessing: And I will bless them that bless thee, and curse him that curseth thee: and in thee shall all families of the earth be blessed.*

Galatians 3:16-18 *Now to Abraham and his seed were the promises made. He saith not, and to seeds, as of many; but as of one, and to thy seed, which is Christ. And this I say, that the covenant, that was confirmed before of God in Christ, the* *law, which was four hundred and thirty years after, cannot disannul, that it should make the promise of none effect. For if the inheritance be of the law, it is no more of promise: but God gave it to Abraham by promise.*

Genesis 22:17-18- That in blessing I will bless thee, and in multiplying I will multiply thy seed as the stars of heaven, and as the sand which is upon the seashore; and thy seed shall possess the gate of his enemies; And in thy seed shall all the nations of the earth be blessed; because thou hast obeyed my voice.

The reasons for the blessing of God go beyond our own personal gratification and comfort. The blessing goes beyond us four and no more, it goes beyond just our immediate family, beyond our local church, organization and nation. It extends to the whole kingdom of God (personal, family, church, communities, and governments). We are blessed to be a blessing. The blessing should overflow our lives and issue a blessing to all we come into contact with.

The blessing was not just one dimensional, but multi-dimensional. It included spiritual blessings, physical blessings, mental blessings, social blessings, and financial blessings. Since we are blessed to be a blessing, all of these blessings should be so abundant in our lives, that it overflows and blesses the lives of others. If we are poor or insufficient in any of these areas, we could not share the blessing with others, or we would only have enough to take care of ourselves. I believe the Lord has come to not only give us life, but life more abundantly.

Economically when we are prosperous in monetary terms such as Bill Cosby, Oprah Winfrey, Bill Gates, Ted Turner and Warren Buffet, we could do more than only advance the kingdom and the gospel of Jesus Christ to the world, but could participate in many philanthropic pursuits to relieve some of the oppression, poverty, and devastation in the world. Our influence could cross borders, and cultures, and penetrate nations that have never heard the good news of Jesus Christ, or the Gospel of the Kingdom. They could see our good works and glorify our Father which is in heaven. Our money should have a mission, we must do good works, be ready to distribute, and willing to communicate.

In Jesus Christ, the seed of Abraham, all families of the earth are blessed. It is of utmost importance that we get this news to all families, that not only are they blessed, but through Jesus Christ our Lord they have been redeemed from poverty, sickness and disease, and from spiritual death. With the infectious nature of blessings you can find that we all have the potential to be blessed for a blessing. It is our obligation to pursue the blessing and grab on to it so we may pass it on to our brethren far and wide.

Luke 6:38- *Give, and it shall be given unto you; good measure, pressed down, and shaken together, and running over, shall men give into* *your bosom. For with the same measure that ye mete withal it shall be measured to you again.*

Ecclesiastes 10:19- *A feast is made for laughter, and wine maketh merry: but money answereth all things.*

Ecclesiastes 7:12- *For wisdom is a defense, and money is a defense: but the excellency of knowledge is that wisdom giveth life to them that have it.*

1 Chronicles 4:10- *And Jabez called on the God of Israel, saying, Oh that thou wouldest bless me indeed, and enlarge my coast, and that thine hand might be with me, and that thou wouldest keep me from evil, that it may not grieve me! And God granted him that which he requested.*

3 John 2- *Beloved, I wish above all things that thou mayest prosper and be in health, even as thy soul prospereth.*

Psalms 1:3- *And he shall be like a tree planted by the rivers of water, that bringeth forth his fruit in his season; his leaf also shall not wither; and whatsoever he doeth shall prosper.*

Deuteronomy 28th Chapter
21 Blessings for Obedience

➢ **1**. God will set you on high above all the other nations of the earth, and all these blessings shall come on you, and overtake you.

➢ **2**. You will be blessed in the city.

➢ **3**. You will be blessed in the field.

➢ **4**. You will have perfect offspring.

➢ **5**. Your crops will be blessed.

➢ **6**. Your cattle will increase.

➢ **7**. Your flocks will increase.

➢ **8**. Your baskets and storehouses will be full of good things.

➢ **9**. You will be blessed in all you undertake.

➢ **10**. You will have complete victory over all your enemies.

➢ **11**. Your land will be abundantly fertile and productive.

➢ **12**. You will be established as a holy people to God.

➢ **13**. You will be a witness and an example to all people on earth.

➢ **14**. All nations will be afraid of you.

➢ **15**. You will be prosperous in goods, in children, in stock, and in crops in all the land.

➢ **16**. The Lord will open to you all His good treasure.

➢ **17**. The heavens will give you rain in due season in all your land.

➢ **18**. The Lord will bless all the work of your hands.

➢ **19**. You will be prosperous enough to lend to nations, and you will not need to borrow from them.

➢ **20**. The Lord shall make you the head, and not the tail.

➢ **21**. You will be above all men and never beneath them.

CHAPTER 10

It's About Time

One of our most precious commodities is time, when it comes down to the four cash flow quadrants; time is the most valuable factor. For an employee who sells their labor and time, most times this keeps an employee away from home approximately a half of a day, for forty years. That type of time consumption keeps folks from minding their own business.

Usually a person starts the first quarter of their working days at 25 years old, and ends at about 65 years old. The first quarter is from 25-35, the second quarter from 35-45, third 45-55, and the fourth from 55-65. In these times there are many people that will still be working past 65 years old because economically they have to. In a poll taken out of 100 people 65 years old, 1 was rich, 4 was wealthy, 5 was still working, 54 was dependent on government and family for support, and 36 were dead.

What would happen if a person stopped working? How long would he or she be able to live at their current comfort level? One way we measure wealth pertains to time. This theory can be summed up by how long a person could live into the future at their current comfort level without working.

People's true assets would be revealed through this theory. The differences between ones liabilities and assets are cleared, and whether they deal in big business or small business. True assets feed you, but liabilities consume you. A true big business owner could leave their business for a year or more, returning to find their business more profitable than when they left it. In contrast, not only would the income of the small business owner be diminished, but the business itself may not survive.

Most people have spent valuable time in the pursuit of earning a living, paying bills, saving for dreams, emergencies, and retirement; these have consumed a large portion of our time (the rat race).

The time factor exponentially increases if a person is self employed. An upstart small business requires about 16 hours per day to stay afloat. As told in the small business quadrant, small business owners must take care of everything that has to do with the business, micro-managing every detail of their prized possession; including payrolls, taxes, insurance, Human resources, and many day to day problems. Most see the self employed or the small business owner as literally buying themselves a job and are hands on due to it being their livelihood. The time they put in depends on whether they are successful or a failure.

Robert Kiyosaki's books "Rich Dad Poor Dad and The Cash Flow Quadrant" refers to the B-I triangle, in which it details that most business' are destined to fail within the first five years regardless of the amount of investment. Both folks in the E (employee) and S (self employee, small business) quadrants time are valuable, but S classers must be smarter and more efficient with their time factor.

B (big business) and I (investors) quadrants time is less imperative to their well being. Big business owners and investors are able to take a hands off approach and let others spend their time to make gains for them. Because of these quadrants use of other people's power, it is considered the most useful of one's time asset. By buying cash flowing assets, Investors transfers other people's time into financial gain. We, especially in the church ought to take advantage of our time assets in the most efficient ways possible.

Ephesians 5:16- *Redeeming the time, because the days are evil.*

The father of time management, Henry Ford the founder of Ford Motor Company; revolutionized industrial business. By implementing the assembly line, Ford vastly improved output while cutting cost. Fords abstract thinking allowed him to democratize the automobile, bringing it to families around the globe. He realized that time maximization could not only benefit his business, but the global community as a whole. Seeing weak points in traditional practices, Ford was able to inspire those around him to think creatively and said that his real mission in life was the making of men.

Although Ford came from a quaint background he used his time and the time of others to its highest potential. Born into poverty Henry Ford achieved only a eighth grade education. Intellectual media ridiculed Fords lack of traditional education branding him as ignorant. Despite their criticisms Ford welcomed naysayers, so that his point of view could be properly understood. Reporters clamored at the opportunity to further point out Fords ill qualities. Seizing the chance, smart alleck journalist trying to question Ford's intelligence asked him questions ranging from financial statistics to the tensile strength of certain metals. Undaunted Ford called in his team one by one to answer these curve ball questionings. Ford did this to prove a point. His time was a valuable asset. He did not have to be a brainiac to realize that the utilization of his many specialists time was much more effective than filling his own head with numbers and information. Fords business structure allowed for the maximization of time. Dumbfounded reporters realized their folly, conceding to Ford's business senses.

By surrounding themselves with professionals, big business owners utilize their time most effectively.

Usually in small business, the owner is the smartest one, but big business owners hire people who are smarter than themselves. So who is the smartest? Investors gain even greater time effectiveness by letting their money work for money.

Time is one thing that you can never get back. Everyone has a limited amount of it. Our mortality dictates that we should use our time in the most efficient way possible. If we use time in the right ways we are one more step closer to financial independence.

CHAPTER 11

Oneness

Jesus' prayer (his high priestly prayer of St. John 17) announced we would be one even as he is one. I believe this prayer must be answered, for we are in the last and glorious days before the rapture of the church – occupy till I come.

We are one body, the body of Christ, the temple of the Holy Ghost. We may be many members, with different functions as the natural body, but we are one in mind and spirit. All parts of the body functions in unison as we are the glory of God, and are fearfully and wondrously made. Simultaneously, Eyes see, ears hear, nerves feel. Circulatory, respiratory, digestion, skeletal, and endocrine systems all operate as one at the same time. One body having the same care, with no schism in the body; if one of our members of our body suffers the whole body suffers. When one member is honored the whole body receives honor.

The gift to the church, the five-fold ministry of Apostles, Prophets, Evangelists, Pastors and Teachers are for the perfecting of the saints, for the work of their ministry, and the edification of the body of Christ. Till we all come into the unity of the faith, and unto the knowledge of the Son God unto a perfect man, unto the measure of the stature of the fullness of Christ. That we henceforth be no more children tossed to and fro and carried about with every wind of doctrine.

God is calling for oneness; it was testified by God concerning the people who were building the tower of Babel back in Old Testament times.

Genesis 11:6- *And the Lord said, Behold, the people is one, and they have all one language; and this they begin to do: and now nothing will be restrained from them, which they have imagined to do*.

Notice the first thing was that the people were one. They were united in, leadership, spirit, mission, vision and teamwork.

The Second thing was that they had one language, they spoke the same thing. The scriptures tell us many times over and over again to speak the same things, walk by the same rule, have the same mind, be on one accord, no division, have the same judgment, one body, one Spirit, one hope, one Lord, one faith, one baptism, one God and father of us all, who is above all, and through all, and in you all, in Him we live and move and have our being, we are the offspring of God. He hath made of one blood all nations of men for to dwell on all the face of the earth, and hath determined the times before appointed, and the bounds of their habitation.

Look at all of the togethers in the scriptures, **THEY GATHERED TOGETHER, THEY SUFFERED TOGETHER, THEY WERE KNOWN TO SING TOGETHER, THEY WENT TO WAR TOGETHER, THEY JOINED TOGETHER, THEY WERE TEMPERED TOGETHER, they assembled together, they dwelled together, they pitched together, they met together, they were called together, they were knit together, they were wrapped together, in a league together, they congregated together, they were purified together, they sang together, they took council together, they were at rest together, they were fashioned together, they were known to stick together, they were joyful together, they consulted together, they compacted together, they lived together, they reasoned together, they stood together, they pleaded together, they could spring up together, drew near together, bowed down together, flowed together, feed together, cry together, they could be brought together, walk together, grow together, be joined together, sit together, agree together, talk together, commune together, they went forth together, they banded together, they planted together, they glorified together, they were perfectly joined together,**

laborers together, workers together, quickened together, framed together, bound together, they built together, were heirs together, elected together, and was made to sit together in heavenly places in Christ Jesus.

Notice in our text that they all had one language meaning they spoke the same thing. We must not contradict one another when we say we can do it. No one should say that we can't. I can do all things through Christ that strengthens me. When we say we are healed, no one should say that we aren't, for by his stripes we are healed. We must speak the same things, since we are speaking spirits, created in the image and likeness of God, and are able to create.

There can yet be unity, without being cookie cutter robots, because God made us diverse, many members yet but one body.

Third and lastly the people began to do something, whatever we put our hands to do will prosper, since we only want to do the right things and work in the name of Jesus, all things are possible.

James 2:26- *For as the body without the spirit is dead, so faith without works is dead also.*

Now God himself comes down to see what is going on, and testifies to the power of unity when mankind is one, and speak the same thing, and begin to do something, that nothing will be retrained from them of what they imagine to do. Now God must get involved.

Genesis 11:7-9- *Go to, let us go down, and there confound their language, that they may not understand one another's speech. So the Lord scattered them abroad from thence upon the face of all the earth: and they left off to build the city. Therefore is the name of it called Babel; because the LORD did there confound the language of all the earth: and from thence did the LORD scatter them abroad upon the face of all the earth.*

The reason that God did this is because he had told them to overspread the earth, not stay in one place, and defy the commandment of God. They wanted to create a one world government, and one world religion that excluded God and promoted humanism. These people were disobedient to the commandment of God, but what about being obedient to God and expanding His Kingdom (rule).

The principle of unity still work. When mankind is one and they speak the same things, and began to do something, nothing is impossible. In New Testament times, now God called the people back again, and changed their language on the day of Pentecost.

Acts 2:1-4 *And when the day of Pentecost was fully come, they were all with one accord in one place. And suddenly there came a sound from heaven as of a rushing mighty wind, and it filled all the house where they were sitting. And there appeared unto them cloven tongues like as of fire, and it sat upon each of them. And they were all filled with the Holy Ghost, and began to speak* *with other tongues, as the Spirit gave them utterance.*

They believed and received the promise. Now we are to go into all the world, and preach the gospel to every creature. Let's do something, since we understand that togetherness is powerful. Use that power.

Acts 1:8- *But ye shall receive power, after that the Holy Ghost is come upon you: and ye shall be witnesses unto me both in Jerusalem, and in all Judaea, and in Samaria, and unto the uttermost part of the earth.*

Philippians 2:13- *For it is God which worketh in you both to will and to do of his good pleasure.*

Philippians 1:6- *Being confident of this very thing, that he which hath begun a good work in you will perform it until the day of Jesus Christ:*

Titus 2:13-14- *Looking for that blessed hope, and the glorious appearing of the great God and our Saviour Jesus Christ; Who gave himself for us, that he might redeem us from all iniquity, and purify unto himself a peculiar people, zealous of good works.*

Chapter 12

Money and Knowledge

Saving and tightening your belt are outdated ways to obtain wealth. It would take a lifetime to achieve a comfortable level of wealth that way. Due to inflation (silent tax) money slowly loses its value over time. Interest rates in banks are too low to overtake inflation (silent tax), thus if you do not invest your money wisely you are losing money by the hour. Money today can be viewed as a type of debt. Its value can be calculated by how many dollars are in circulation and the overall confidence the world have in our ability to pay back our debt

In 1971, President Richard Nixon severed the dollar from the gold standard (Every since then the dollar has become a currency, and have been losing value through inflation.) There were pros and cons to this move. The new gold-less currency could be better manipulated, and was thought to have a more constant value. Even though silver and gold is the only real money that increases with inflation, while most paper currencies go to zero. Even the American dollar has lost 95% of its value due to inflation (silent tax) and it won't be long before it loses the other 5%.

A drawback pertains to increasing of the national debt that we pass on to future generations, and the increase of the inflation trend. Food and energy are not counted in inflation because of manipulation. Government has to increase the amount of benefits in entitlement programs to include inflation (cost of living); this is one reason why food and energy are not counted in inflation. But we know that the cost of food and energy has increased dramatically.

In the 1970's the government was stuck in stagflation. Stagflation is an economic condition where inflation is above economic growth. In this situation if the government takes actions to lower inflation the economy would suffer, while if they take steps to improve the economy; by increasing spending, inflation would rise.

The Federal Reserve Bank is what has oversight of the dollar. The government has little authority over the Federal Reserve Bank, it can be viewed as a money cartel controlled by wealthy bankers and powerful investors. The fed is able to print money out of thin air to buy bonds and instruments that the government creates (literally trillions of dollars). To pay bills, prop up the stock market, stimulate the economy, bail out big banks and businesses, to take care of entitlement programs that are broke or underfunded.

Since the dollar is not tied to something tangible, the government can print money out of thin air. Governments print more money to spur economic growth, but it is a delicate balance between growth and inflation. The bill gets passed on to the taxpayers and future generations. This is one of the reasons why it is not smart to save money, when there is so much debt and inflation. We must learn how to use debt to our advantage, since money is debt.

The over printing of currency is best illustrated by post World War I Germany. Incompetent proxy government officials tried to bring themselves out of the great depression by simply printing more money. This might have seemed like a good idea, but sadly it had devastating effects. The cost of everyday items rose so that for a loaf of bread a wheel barrel of useless money was needed. In that economy the wheel barrel was more valuable than all the cash in it.

In more recent history, Zimbabwe had similar problems where the people were charged millions of dollars of their zero sum paper money to purchase three eggs. Corrupt dictators and governmental officials gave themselves truckloads of cash thinking it would lead to a platinum lifestyle. Unfortunately this move led to the destabilization of the entire economy and the increased suffering of the Zimbabwean people. I remember a story of a preacher that went to

Zimbabwe to preach, he received millions of dollars as an offering. His travel companions thought they had arrived on to the world's stage as mega millionaires. They soon learned that one million dollar was not much money at all in that currency.

Due to many similar factors, nations and investors are losing confidence in the United States and the dollar as the reserve currency. The downgrade of the U.S. credit rating is one indicator of falling confidence. While other nations rise in the worlds eyes such as China and India, The U.S. economy is being squeezed even further.

In this economy savers are losers because inflation (silent tax) is higher than interest rates. The interest rate for savers is about 1%. It is set this low because of our need for investment. The incentives have been taken out of savings by decreasing interest rates, and also to push everyone into buying mutual funds through the 401k plan.

Since most individuals do not view themselves as investors, they continue to save. This is an ideal situation for banks. Banks use patrons saved money for lending. They can lend up to ten or more times the amount of saved money they have in their possession. The banks are allowed to charge whatever interest rates best suits them, resulting in banks especially big banks winning; while the rest of us lose. Instead of saving we must look into cash flowing assets, this is turning money into gold. Since money is now a currency, it must keep moving; when it is stagnant the value diminishes.

The power bestowed by God is an awesome power, the power to make our own path in the world. Wealth is not given to us; rather we have the power to obtain wealth. Wealth creation strategies and vehicles are ready and available for the people of God to pursue. A covenant can be established through the plans that are allotted to each of us.

Instead of giving people fish, we must teach people how to fish for themselves. The easy way is to just give them the fish and they go on their way, but we have the heart, mind, and spirit of Christ. He emphasized the importance of teaching your fellow man.

John 6:26-27- *Jesus answered them and said, Verily, verily, I say unto you, Ye seek me, not because ye saw the miracles, but because ye did eat of the loaves, and were filled. Labour not for the meat which perisheth, but for the meat which endureth unto everlasting life, which the Son of man shall give unto you: for him hath God the Father sealed.*

Visiting cities far and wide, Jesus taught regardless of where or to whom. Teaching of valuable life lessons can be imprinted in a person's heart which will stick with them through the ages. The hunger that we all feel does not mean we should go to McDonalds; the food that we long for is mental and spiritual knowledge. Without the guiding aspect of wisdom our actions are folly and uninspired. Scripture says,

Hosea 4:6- *My people are destroyed for lack of knowledge: because thou hast rejected knowledge, I will also reject thee, that thou shalt be no priest to me: seeing thou hast forgotten the law of thy God, I will also forget thy children.*

And,

Proverbs 4:7- *Wisdom is the principle thing; therefore get wisdom: and with all thy getting get understanding.*"

Jeremiah 3:15- *And I will give you pastors according to mine heart, which shall feed you with knowledge and understanding.*

Sometimes the simplest lessons carry the most weight. Thinking of lessons I learned in kindergarten, where we were taught fairy tales. In retrospect these stories were not simply about princesses, knights, and giants. Deeper meaning ingrained little bits of wisdom into growing minds. Remember the story of the three little pigs. They were sent off into the world determined to make their lot in life. On their own they constructed three different types of houses. The first pig built his house with straw, the second built her house with wood, and the third pig built with bricks. The wolf huffed and puffed and blew the first two pig's house down. The wolf was not able to blow the third pig's house down because it was built with a stable material, bricks. Now for a The Word of God, Jesus said in

St. Matthew 7:24-27 - *"Therefore whosoever heareth these sayings of mine, and doeth them, I*

will liken him unto a wise man, which built his house upon a rock: And the rain descended, and the floods came, and the winds blew, and beat upon that house; and it fell not: for it was founded upon a rock. And every one that heareth these sayings of mine, and doeth them not, shall be likened unto a foolish man, which built his house upon the sand: And the rain descended, and the floods came, and the winds blew, and beat upon that house; and it fell: and great was the fall of it."

The floods and the winds do not exempt anyone, so it behooves one to be prepared. In view of our financial situation, a financial storm is on the horizon. The dark clouds of unemployment and inflation (silent tax) are looming ever so closely ready to swallow the earth whole. Just as God warned Noah concerning the coming flood, causing him to move with fear (purpose). Noah prepared an ark of safety for himself, his family, and for all that would heed his ordained knowledge. There is an economic storm coming. Jesus said that as it was in the days of Noah so shall it be in his days. The time for us to build our arks is at hand.

Without the guiding power of God-given knowledge, our economic state has worsened. Many have lost their pensions, losing the ability to safely retire.   By the way, one of the greatest fears is running out of money and/or not having enough to live comfortable while in retirement.   401k's wither away as the stock market sputters making retirement that much more unreachable.

A great number of people are now reaching retirement age. These are the "baby boomers" [between 1945 and 1964 seventy six million (76,000,000) American children were born], they are the children of the men and women who won WWII and they now are ready to reap from a long life of work. These people are now pulling their assets out of their 401k plan and are required by law to pay their taxes at the earned income rate. As more and more people draw money out of the stock markets, than contributing, it is predicted by Robert Kiyosaki, in his book "Prophesy", that there will be another historical major stock market crash. With a crash in the market, panic would ensue resulting in people withdrawing their money regardless of a penalty (10% plus current income tax rate).

Unemployment is high and good paying jobs are scarce especially in our inner cities. The youth are graduating from college and cannot find their dream job. Their student loans have accumulated a mountain of debt for them and their parents, which must be paid. In more and more cases students are unable to cope once entering the workforce. There are a growing number of recent graduates that are jobless and are forced to move back home with their parents. The growing trend is that there are two, three, and sometimes four generations under one roof. Even some new homes are built using the multi-generational model.

In a surprising high rate of occurrence many youth; disparaged with their economic potential, choose a life on the street rather than formal education. This deviation has resulted in a record number of youth either deceased or incarcerated. Sadly the black community has been hit the hardest by this epidemic. Due to the ingrained discrimination in our society, especially towards ex- criminals, the black community usually draws the short straw in regards to access and opportunity.

The prison system has turned into an industrial complex rather than a rehabilitation center. Big business controls the prison population. With the availability of cheap labor through the prison system, our society teeters on its own morality in regards to forced labor. I emphasize the importance of financial wisdom because this pain and hardship can be avoided. A proper financial education can shed light on an otherwise shady world.

The good old days of when there was a good job with benefits are a thing of the past. Without knowledge most people are unable to see the change from this generation from the last. There was a time when you could stay on one job all of your working days until retirement. Now people usually change jobs three or four and sometimes more times during their working years. Also many people work two or more jobs in these days that we live in, to make ends meet.

We must give the knowledge to know how to find the fish. We must give knowledge to cast out the nets. We must give the knowledge to reel them in. With the passage of knowledge we all grow spiritually and financially. We must all provide, and with the supply and wisdom of God we provide for all our needs and more. Armed with knowledge and the power of

God you can arise and arrive. Do not settle for just a fish, but strive for knowledge that will propel you into a new financial revolution.

Jesus said in

St. Luke 4:18-19-- *The Spirit of the Lord is upon me, because he hath anointed me to preach the gospel to the poor; he hath sent me to heal the brokenhearted, to preach deliverance to the captives, and recovering of sight to the blind, to set at liberty them that are bruised, To preach the acceptable year of the Lord*.

St. Matthew 11:12- *And from the days of John the Baptist until now the kingdom of heaven, suffereth violence, and the violent take it by force.*

CHAPTER 13

How Can They Preach

Romans 10:13-15 – *For whosoever shall call upon the name of the Lord shall be saved. How then shall they call upon him in whom they have not believed? And how shall they believe in him of whom they have not heard? And how shall they hear without a preacher? And how shall they preach, except they be sent? As it is written, how beautiful are the feet of them that preach the gospel of peace and bring glad tidings of good things.*

Not only is this a scripture concerning the preacher's call to the ministry, because we are all called to the ministry. When Our Lord Jesus Christ was giving the great Vision for the Kingdom, He said

"But ye shall receive power after that the Holy Ghost is come upon you; and ye shall be witnesses unto me both in Jerusalem, and in all Judea, and in Samaria, and unto the uttermost part of the earth. Even though the Lord gives specific clear vision, and territory, and target audiences to specific ministries, yet it is contained in the great vision to go ye into all the world and preach the gospel to every creature. He that believeth and is baptized shall be saved, he that believeth not shall be damned.

Also even the fivefold ministry's aim and mission is not to create an elite group of individuals, but to be a gift to the church to perfect the saints for the work of their ministries that the body of Christ might be edified and grow. Remember Jesus said in the book of Revelation, that I hate the deeds of the Nicolaitanes. This group exalted themselves into an elite group and separated the people into the laity. They were not a sect, but a party in the Church who were trying to establish a "Priestly Order." Probably trying to model the Church after the Old Testament order of Priests, Levites, and common people. We are all a kingdom of priests, (a royal priesthood) represented by our great high priest Jesus Christ, a priesthood greater than the Levites and the Aaronic order. Thou art a priest forever after the order of Melchesidek.

So when the scripture says how can they preach, this also speaks about financing and sending those who could go to preach the gospel. How can they preach except they be sent, is also an economic statement that we should send them (the missionaries) with our finances until we cover the whole earth. Yes, cover the whole earth with the gospel. It is true that you cannot replace the anointing and the Spirit with money, for no man can come to me Jesus said, except the Father which hath sent me draw him. Zechariah said, Not by might, nor by power, but by my spirit, saith the LORD of hosts.

When Jesus stood in the synagogue it was delivered to him the book of Esaias (Isaiah) the prophet, he opened the book, found the place where it was written, and read,

Luke 4:18- *The Spirit of the Lord is upon me, because he hath anointed me to preach the gospel to the poor...*

This is part of the gospel, and the first anointing that we receive. If we get this first anointing right, then there would be fewer broken hearts, captives, blinded eyes, and bruised people. It is true that most of the divorce rate (50%) is caused by finance. Then we must preach the acceptable year of the Lord, the year of the Lord's release (Jubilee), the favor of the Lord. After being born again, the word tells us in

Matthew 6:33- *But seek ye first the kingdom of God, and his righteousness; and all these things shall be added unto you.*

We must understand that we are the righteousness of God. Righteousness is a gift that was given to us by God.

Romans 5:17- *For if by one man's offence death reigned by one; much more they which receive abundance of grace and of the gift of righteousness shall reign in life by one, Jesus Christ.)*

2 Corinthians 5:21- *For he hath made him to be sin for us, who knew no sin; that we might be made the righteousness of God in him.*

1 Corinthians 1:30-31- *But of him are ye in Christ Jesus, who of God is made unto us wisdom, and righteousness, and sanctification, and redemption: That, according as it is written, He that glorieth, let him glory in the Lord.*

You must learn how to live in the kingdom and learn how to obtain the benefits of being a son of God and the righteousness of God (we are not sinners saved by grace). If you are the poor, your giving may be severely limited. You are invested with power to get wealth.

When Israel was delivered from Egypt, after over four hundred years of slavery, they spoiled the Egyptians, in other words they took the riches of Egypt. These riches were not just for the Israelites to say we are rich, but it was in their possession for the kingdom, to build the House of God. They had more than enough to build the Tabernacle in the wilderness. They had the presence of God by day in a cloud and at night by a pillar of fire, they had silver and gold (real money), precious stones, fabrics, bronze, woods, cattle, livestock, servants, furs and leathers, oils, spices and everything necessary to make the tabernacle after the pattern shown to Moses in the mount (heaven).

By the way the church in the wilderness was one of the most expensive (valuable) buildings ever constructed, about the size of a city block. The people brought so much material for its construction that Moses had to tell them to stop bringing an offering (suppose we could do that). They were able to give and had plenty for themselves. They were not poor anymore. They were delivered from poverty. We are also delivered from poverty.

John Avanzini in his book Rich God Poor God, he stated the mindset that must be destroyed was seeing God as poor and must receive offerings to support His work. We must see Him as rich and able to give provision to support His vision. Our God is El Shaddia (the God who is more than enough).

Any one speaking concerning money is immediately dubbed as a prosperity preacher because many think that financial education has no place in the church or the preacher is trying to get their hands on the members' hard earned dollar. Please rethink this narrow train of thought. If we are to cover the earth with the gospel, money is needed, as money answers all things. Who is to give it? The people of God are to give. The Israelites did not go to the other people in the surrounding areas and ask for the materials to build the Tabernacle in the Wilderness. No! They had it to give.

Use wisdom, knowledge and understanding to move into financial freedom. Wisdom to know who you are, and the knowledge to use financial education to excel in business and understanding to accept your rights as sons of God to have dominion in the earth and advance the kingdom of God.

It is probable for one or two of our ministries to be on television, or launch oversea ministries, while our other ministries support them (how can they preach except they be sent). It takes an enormous amount of money for ministry, and we must start to think beyond tithes and offerings (this we ought to do). Jesus said occupy till I come. Do Business. Whatever your gift is, it was given to you by God himself, and our privilege is to occupy and increase till he comes. Everyone is given opportunity. I must work the work of him that sent me while it is day, for the night cometh when no man can work. Behold, I come quickly.

Philippians 4:19- *But my God shall supply all your need according to his riches in glory by Christ Jesus.*

St. Matthew 6:33- *But seek ye first the kingdom of God, and his righteousness; and all these things shall be added unto you.*

The whole body of Christ are kings and priests.

Revelation 5:10- *And hast made us unto our God kings and priests: and we shall reign on the earth.*

The ABC's of Affluence

A) Authority, all possibility, affluence, absolute, abundance

B) Belief, better and best, principle of the highest first, go first class,

C) Charity, communication, carefreeness

D) Demand and supply

E) Exalting in the success of others

F) In every failure is the seed of success

G) Gratitude and generosity, God, goal

H) Happiness and hope, humility, humanity

I) Intent, unchangeable decision, single mindedness

J) Judge not

K) Knowledge, organizing power, awareness

L) Love and luxury, love your neighbor as yourself

M) Making money for others

N) No to negativity

O) Opportunity, open honesty, organizing

P) Purpose, potentiality, prayer

Q) Question outside authority

R) Receiving is as necessary as giving

S) Service, sowing

T) Tithing , talent

U) Understanding unity

V) Values

W) Wealth consciousness without worries

X) Expressing honest appreciation for all who help us

Y) Youth renewed, vigor

Z) Zest and zeal for life

CHAPTER 14

I Have A Vision

Habakkuk 2:2-4- *And the Lord answered me, and said, Write the vision, and make it plain upon tables, that he may run that readeth it. For the vision is yet for an appointed time, but at the end it shall speak, and not lie: though it tarry, wait for it; because it will surely come, it will not tarry. Behold, his soul which is lifted up is not upright in him; but the just shall live by his faith.*

Joel 2:28-29- *And it shall come to pass afterward, that I will pour out my spirit upon all flesh; and your sons and your daughters shall prophesy, your old men shall dream dreams, your young men shall see visions: And also upon the servants and upon the handmaids in those days will I pour out my spirit.*

Proverbs 29:18- *Where there is no vision, the people perish: but he that keepeth the law, happy is he.*

Romans 1:17- *For therein is the righteousness of God revealed from faith to faith: as it is written. The just shall live by faith.*

After completing my writings, I thought the book was finished. I sent it by e-mail to a few people who could read it and send me their input, honest and open communication, positive criticism, endorsements and etc.

The only feedback that I received came from my oldest brother Johnny. He said that he loved the book and noted that I had a lot of information, but there was something missing, my testimony, my passion and my vision.

He continued writing and questioned whether I had ever thought about tithing $1000 dollars per week. Have you ever envisioned speaking before a packed auditorium with overflow rooms filled to capacity? Have you ever seen yourself able to fly yourself and your family to any destination in the world? Have you ever imagined staying in a 5 star hotel and ordering up room service? Have you ever thought of giving away the luxury vehicle that you purchased last year? What about providing a new home for your Mother with a live-in maid? Have you ever thought of providing the money for your grand children, nieces and nephews to go to the school of their choice? How about someone coming to your home to tailor your suits and your wife's dresses? How about having a store close its doors to the public so you can let some needy children shop at their leisure?

I wrote back and said, great insight, you got me to really thinking now, so, Ready, Fire, Aim. You see I had asked Johnny to teach me how to close a sale, because he has been an excellent salesman for most of his life, and I wanted to share this information with my readers. Johnny is a master salesman, what he wrote in his response is what I needed to close the deal. I realized I had some more writing to do because I do think of all these things and more. I always wanted to create a magic account for my mother, mother in law, and my wife that would never run out of money, no matter how much they spent, and no matter what they purchased. When playing the game cash flow, which was created by the Rich Dad Company, the first thing you must do is choose a dream. The first one who lands on their dream after getting out of the rat race and onto the fast track wins the game, or the first to earn $50,000 additional passive income by buying businesses.

The dream I always choose is A Gift of Faith, (Your religious organization is growing by leaps and bounds. New buildings are needed. You donate $175,000) and my wife, Alyce, always choose dinner with the President (Buy a table for 10 friends to dine with the president at a gala ball for visiting dignitaries from around the world $100,000).

But while we are on our way to achieving our wealthy place, and reaching our dreams, we purchase many more dreams along the way. Such as an African Photo Safari ($100,000), a mini-farm in the city ($150,000), Cruise the Mediterranean on a private yacht ($100,000). Capitalist's Peace Corps (set up entrepreneurial business schools in third world nations, instructors are business people donating their knowledge and time $200,000), South Sea Island Fantasy (pampered in luxury for two full months, relax, unwind in warm waters, deserted beaches, and romantic nights $100,000), A Kid's Library (add a wing to your city's library donated to young writers, and artists. Art celebrities visit often to support your work $175,000), Golf around the world (take three friends on a first class, five-star resort tour to play the fifty best golf courses in the world $150,000). Be a jet setter (have your own personal jet available for one year to whisk you away whenever and wherever your heart desires $250,000). 7 Wonders of the World (Go by plane, boat, bike, camel, canoe and limo to the 7 wonders of the world. First class luxury all the way $200,000). We also buy the dreams: Run for mayor $125,000, private fishing cabin on a Montana Lake $100,000, a stock market for kids (Fund a business & investment school for young capitalist's, teaching them the basics of business. School includes a mini stock exchange ran by the students $120,000). Pro Team Box Seats (License a 12 person private skybox booth with food and beverage service at your favorite team's stadium $200,000).

While buying businesses, and landing on your main dream these are some of the dreams that you encounter along the way. In the game I usually buy them all. This is teaching me how to be generous and give back as well as to enjoy myself and my family and have the money to do it. Choices, you need to have choices. Seek ye first the Kingdom of God and his righteousness, and all these things shall be added unto you. What about winning a million souls into the kingdom?

The reason why we play games that assimilate the real life experience is because we must get this into our spirits. We retain 90% of what we say and do. That is doing the real thing, simulating the real experience, doing a dramatic presentation. This is active learning. Although the way school is normally taught is through reading, and hearing a lecture, which the retention rate is only 10%, and 20% respectively, the passive way of learning. That is why the game cash flow cost $199.99, because you are actually assimilating the real thing and the game is true to life.

The object of the game is to get out of the rat race (going from pay check to paycheck) and on to the fast track, by building up your passive income to be greater than your expenses. Once you do this you are allowed onto the fast track as an accredited investor, and are able to buy businesses and some of these dreams that I wrote about above. You can practice with play money while gaining the experience to be a true investor. It is teaching you something that you will never learn in school. Also you are learning accounting, the relationship between the balance sheet and the income statement, and how to build passive income, and how to spot a good opportunity, big or small (priceless).

Dr Martin Luther King Jr. pointed to the future when he said I have a dream. Vision is a clear mental image of a preferable future imparted by God to his chosen leader and is based upon an accurate understanding of God, self and circumstances. This picture is internalized and personal; it is not somebody else's view of the future, but one that uniquely belongs to you. Eventually, you will have to paint that mental portrait for others if you wish the vision to materialize in your life, in the life of others, in the church and in business. Please note that the vision must be clear, and not a fuzzy prospective.

Vision is never about accepting and maintaining the status quo. It is about stretching reality to extend beyond the existing state. Vision is yet required when you are already in a good position. For example, you may have a growing church and may be successful, but to take the church where God wants you to, you still must have vision. In your personal life, you may have a good job making good money, but you still need vision for your future.

We can no longer rely upon random circumstances and hope that the results are better than what have existed before. The definition of insanity is doing the same thing and expecting a different result. We can assert control over our environment based on God's empowerment and direction and make a better future.

In conclusion, I have been involved in several businesses using the network marketing model. Many feel that network marketing is a pyramid scheme or scam, however most of corporate America is a pyramid, because those at the bottom never rise to the top (meaning the workers) whereas, in network marketing your job is to pull others up, making it a true equality business. However many big businesses are now using the network marketing model. Also it is not a get rich quick scheme, but it requires diligence and commitment. We have used the forty year plan and worked hard, why not work diligently for four years to at least replace our current incomes, and at the most become very wealthy. Many of the financial gurus, along with Robert Kiyosaki and Donald Trump had suggested that if they had it to do over again, would do network marketing first before entering into real estate, paper assets, commodities and other businesses.

I have never been immune to hard work, and having an entrepreneurial spirit, even from a child I would do whatever my hands found to do. I collected pop bottles; I cut grass, shoveled snow, raked leaves, sold lemonade, opened the garage doors for neighbors, went to the store for the neighbors, and took out their trash. I have had paper routes, and summer jobs, worked as a plumber when I was a teenager, painted houses, washed walls, painted fences, have been a chauffeur, worked in the party store, the grocery store, and at McDonalds. Then I worked and retired from Ford Motor Company with a defined pension for the rest of my life.

I have pastored a church and held many key positions within my church organization. We have opened other businesses; in all this I still see something more, the more being passive income. Instead of working for money, now is the time to let money work for me. We had been taught to work hard for money.

God casted a vision for us and our future, before the foundation of the world He had a plan for us. God saves the whole man. He came to recreate our spirits, save our souls (mind, will, and emotions), heal our bodies, and make them the temple of the Holy Ghost. He has made us his witnesses unto the uttermost parts of the earth. Moreover, he came to empower our lives, to meet all our needs. He also prepared a place for us in heaven, and hath raised us up together, and made us to sit together in heavenly places in Christ Jesus (the Anointed One and his anointing), called us to be kings and priest that we may reign with him.

God is concerned about our finances as well as our souls, so we should be concerned also. Remember the servants with the talents. Let's take what talents/money that is given to us and increase it and God will increase it the more (but God giveth the increase). First and foremost we must be good stewards. We must be honest and have integrity in all we do.

I was introduced to network marketing (an industry with over 300 billion dollars a year and growing and that has been around for over 50 years). I saw and met many people that grew their finances to well over $10,000 a month, and some that at that time had incomes of over $250,000 per month. I purposed in my heart to take this to my people, my family and my church family. I presented it to church organizations, school PTA's, family reunions, and even went back to Ford to my old work collogues.

The plan was that all the members would come in groups and work together as one to create wealth for the groups and the individual. My idea was that a group of people working together as one could quickly bring increase to all. And when we were successful, we could bring this to other large groups, and church organizations, family reunions, etc. Network marketing is not the only way but a very good vehicle to financial freedom and wealth. There are many ways and plans that God will give to you to achieve the goal of occupying till he come (do business). The solution is not to fear the plan, the people and wealth but to embrace and move to the next paradigm. Gifts and talents comes from God and He expect us to increase with His empowerment. Let us be diligent to incorporate financial knowledge to work while it is day for the night cometh when no man can work. It is time to acknowledge God for direction and He will direct your path.

The traditions that have been taught concerning money, down through the years has been very challenging and trying, even though they were good for the time. Traditions like, go to school so you can find a good job with benefit, work hard for the money in a traditional setting, seek for job security, save money, get out of debt, don't take risks, trust no one when it comes to money. We have been down all these avenues and survived. Remember there is Egypt (land of not enough), the wilderness (land of just enough) and then there is the Promise Land over across Jordan (land of more than enough) the latter is where we want to be. What a journey we have taken and is still on the move. Many are refusing change, yet, I will keep the faith that there are some Joshua's and Caleb's that will catch the vision of Kingdom Business 101 and are willing to go against the norm. There is a promise land that flows with milk and honey. It is so very near. Go up at once and possess it, we must go together as one. Even though we may already be in the Promised Land in most areas of our lives, there is yet more possessing that must be accomplished. Arm yourselves with financial knowledge and conquer your fears and step into Kingdom Business and Occupy till He come. We need a Gideon's Army (300).

"THE PEOPLE THAT DO KNOW THEIR GOD SHALL BE STRONG, AND DO EXPLOITS."

References

1) The Holy Bible King James Version all scriptures and scripture references

2) Kiyosaki, Robert/ Lechter, Sharon. "Rich Dad Poor Dad" author, CPA
Copyright 1997, 1998 Warner Books

3) Kiyosaki, Robert/ Lechter, Sharon. "Rich Dad Poor Dad Cashflow Quadrant, Rich Dad Guide to Financial Freedom" author CPA
Copyright 1998, 1999 Warner Books

4) Kiyosaki, Robert/ Lechter, Sharon. "Rich Dad's Prophecy" Why the Biggest Stock Market Crash in History is Still Coming.....And How You Can Prepare Yourself
Copyright 2002 Warner Books

5) Tenney, Tommy. "God's Dream Team a Call to Unity"
Copyright 1999 Regal Book

6) Chopra, Deepak MD. "Creating Affluence"
The A-to –Z to a Richer Life", ABC's of Affluence
Copyright 1993, 1998 Amber-Allen Publishing/New World Library

7) Avanzini, John. "Rich God Poor God," Your Perception Changes Everything,
Copyright 2001 International Faith Center, inc.

8) Rabbi Daniel Lapin, "Thou Shall Prosper" Ten Commandments for Making Money

Copyright 2002 John Wiley & Sons, Inc

9) Clarence Larkin. "The Book of Revelation" A study of
The Last Prophetic Book of Holy Scripture
Copyright 1919 Published by the Rev. Clarence Larkin
Estate

To Order and Contact

Dr. Marcus A. Sheffield

Email: masheffield7@yahoo.com

Or

alsheff1@yahoo.com

Also available to order

A NEW DAY

by

Alyce L. Sheffield

Uncover your purpose and step into destiny. This book gives great insight on the will and plan of God that is unique for your life. It is both in great depth, but also in simplicity. It enlightens and provokes you to move by the divine design that is set.

A New Day illustrates to the average person, that they themselves are of great value to God and that God is very much interested in the destiny of their lives. His plan and his path are set before you, but you must take time to listen, hear and follow his directions; for the steps of a good man are ordered by the Lord. As you read, a surge of exhilaration will be unleashed in your heart in anticipation of what your new day holds.